WORKING EFFECTIVELY WITH
INDIGENOUS PEOPLES®

ALSO BY BOB JOSEPH
21 Things You May Not Know About the Indian Act

Bob Joseph *and* Cynthia F. Joseph

WORKING EFFECTIVELY WITH INDIGENOUS PEOPLES®

INDIGENOUS
RELATIONS
PRESS

Copyright © 2017 by Indigenous Corporate Training

All rights reserved. No part of this book may be reproduced, stored in a retrieval system or transmitted, in any form or by any means, without the prior written consent of the publisher or a licence from The Canadian Copyright Licensing Agency (Access Copyright). For a copyright licence, visit www.accesscopyright.ca or call toll free to 1-800-893-5777.

Indigenous Relations Press
www.ictinc.ca
Port Coquitlam BC

ISBN 978-0-9781628-5-6 (paperback)
ISBN 978-0-9781628-6-3 (ebook)

Produced by Page Two
www.pagetwostrategies.com
Cover and interior design by Naomi MacDougall
Printed and bound in Canada by Friesens

19 20 21   5 4 3

We dedicate this book to Reconciliation.

CONTENTS

PREFACE

IN WRITING THIS book, I have endeavoured to create a tool that truly is applicable wherever there are colonized Indigenous Peoples. This book originally started as a collection of stapled speaking notes that I used as a foundation for a training course of the same name and a training course that I have, over the course of time, delivered to thousands of people. Those stapled speaking notes additionally evolved into a book, now in its fourth edition. With each new edition, we strive to continuously improve and augment the content.

> Having recently completed training with Indigenous Corporate Training, I'm pleased to see the materials and supporting information book updated to address the evolving nature of relationships, modern treaties, the evolving legal climate, and shifts in engagement and consultation activities when working with First Nations. Having taken this course years ago, the new material is valuable in understanding the evolution of First Nations' application of rights and title cases across Canada's legal system.
> CHRISTINE BOEHRINGER

In my capacity as a trainer, I have the great privilege to meet people who want to learn how to work effectively with Indigenous Peoples. It is my sincere hope that this book will increase readers' Indigenous awareness and cross-cultural understanding, and more importantly, take them a step beyond Indigenous awareness to applying the practical hints, tips, and suggestions in their personal and professional lives.

The book is laid out in a linear timeline format and presents multiple perspectives. It is not designed to convince you of what is right or wrong, but rather to show how different people view a situation, issue, concern, or period in history. It provides a review of historical events and their relation to the present economic environment; explores critical issues of taxation, housing, and education; and provides insight into how working with Indigenous Peoples can enhance your career and business.

Some of you will read this book from this page forward, beginning to end; others will use it as a reference. The book is designed to suit either approach.

More information about Indigenous Corporate Training Inc., our on-site and open-to-the-public Training Weeks can be found on our website (www.ictinc. ca). On our website, you will also find links to sign up for our monthly *Indigenous Relations* newsletter and to our growing library of ebooks that are free for you to download.

We believe that by sharing knowledge and information through this book, our training, blog, and free resources, we can make the world a better place for Indigenous and non-Indigenous people.

Gilakasla
Bob Joseph
Cynthia F. Joseph

NOTES ON TERMINOLOGY

IN THIS FOURTH edition, we make the significant change from Aboriginal to Indigenous, which is reflected in its title: *Working Effectively with Indigenous Peoples*®. This is a momentous change that reflects that the relationship between Indigenous Peoples in Canada and non-Indigenous Canadians, and all levels of government, are on the doorstep of a significant change. The federal government, in 2016, made the move to replace Aboriginal with Indigenous in government communications, thereby turning the handle to open the door to return relations to the nation-to-nation relationship which dates back to 1763 when the *Royal Proclamation* was signed by King George III. At the time of this publication, governments are in a state of flux on the usage of Indigenous or Aboriginal.

Throughout the book, we will generally use the term "Aboriginal Peoples" to indicate the collective group of people who hold various rights and obligations under provisions of the *Indian Act* and section 35 of the Canadian *Constitution Act, 1982*. Additionally, we use it in reference to the census, in quotes and the names of reports.

We use the term "Indigenous Peoples" as the collective term for First Nation, Inuit, and Métis peoples who live in Canada.

In situations where we refer to those individuals of a specific ancestry, i.e. First Nation, Inuit, or Métis, we will refer to them by that name; otherwise they are included within the term Indigenous Peoples.

While there are legal reasons for the continued use of the term "Indian"—such as in the *Indian Act*, and the term is used by the Government of Canada when making references to this particular group of Indigenous Peoples—usage of the term is considered by many to be derogatory and has been largely replaced by Indigenous Peoples. So, we use Indian when it's appropriate for the era we are writing about.

It is for this reason that we only refer to individual First Nation people (one of many preferred terms) when there are legal reasons to do so.

Here are some clarifying definitions and tips on usage that will come in handy with your communications with and about Indigenous Peoples:

Aboriginal Peoples

The collective noun is used in the *Constitution Act, 1982* and includes the Indian (or First Nations), Inuit, and Métis Peoples, so legally it will always have a place at the terminology table.

CAN:
- Use interchangeably with First Peoples
- Use interchangeably with First Nations
- Use interchangeably with Indigenous Peoples

CAUTION:
- If using interchangeably with First Nations, note that some First Nations prefer not to be called Aboriginal Peoples
- If using this, it should always be Aboriginal Peoples together as opposed to Aboriginal or Aboriginals

First Nation(s)

First Nation is a term used to identify Indigenous peoples of Canada who are neither Métis nor Inuit. This term came into common usage in the 1970s to replace the term "Indian" and "Indian band," which many found offensive. First Nations people includes both status and non-status Indians, so there's a need to be careful with its usage, especially if in reference to programs that are specifically for status-Indians.

There is no legal definition for First Nation and it is acceptable as both a noun and a modifier.

CAN:
- Use to refer to a single band or the plural First Nations for many bands
- Use "First Nation community" as a respectful alternative phrase
- Use instead of "Indian" when referring to an individual

CAUTION:
- If using interchangeably with Aboriginal Peoples as some First Nations people don't like the term Aboriginal Peoples
- If using interchangeably with First Nations as some may have more preference for Indigenous Peoples. For example, First Nation communities in Ontario have expressed publicly and politically that they prefer Indigenous Peoples

Indian

"Indian" is the legal identity of an Indigenous person who is registered under the *Indian Act*.

One story about the origin of the term "Indian" dates back to Christopher Columbus who mistakenly thought he had reached the East Indies, so referred to the people in the lands he visited as "indios" which is Spanish for Indian.

CAN:
- Use in direct quotations
- Use when citing titles of books, works of art, etc.
- Use in discussions of history where necessary for clarity and accuracy
- Use in discussions of some legal/constitutional matters requiring precision in terminology
- Use in discussions of rights and benefits provided on the basis of "Indian" status
- Use in statistical information collected using these categories (e.g., the Census)[1]

CAUTION:
- If using in front of individuals as some may deem it is derogatory and outdated and take issue with it.

Indigenous Peoples

A collective noun for First Nations, Inuit, and Métis, and is growing in popularity in Canada.

CAN:
- Use interchangeably with First Peoples
- Use interchangeably with First Nations
- Use interchangeably with Aboriginal Peoples

CAUTION:
- If using interchangeably with First Nations as some may have more preference for Indigenous Peoples. For example, First Nation communities in Ontario have expressed publicly and politically that they prefer Indigenous Peoples

- For definitions of Inuit and Métis, please see Glossary.
- When we refer to the *Indian Act*, unless otherwise noted, it is the current 1985 version, RSC, c 1-5.

Part I: Indigenous

Awareness

A. PRE-CONTACT NATIONS

Scientific and Indigenous Perspectives of the "New World"

There has been much discussion in the scientific community about how and when Indigenous Peoples populated the Americas. One prevailing theory is that Indigenous Peoples arrived by crossing a land bridge sometime around the end of the last ice age, 10,000 to 12,000 years ago. This theory holds that people from Asia migrated into the area that is now the Bering Strait to populate North and South America. More recent scientific research suggests that North and South America were populated by continuous waves of migration over a period of time that extends well beyond the last ice age. This more recent research also indicates that, due to glacial ice, the land bridge may have been impassable up until 12,000 years ago, which doesn't explain how North America became inhabited prior to this time. Exactly how the Americas were populated prior to European contact has not been definitively determined.

Most cultures, including Indigenous cultures, hold creationism as an explanation of how people came to populate the world. If an Indigenous person were asked his or her idea of how their ancestors came to live in the Americas, the answer would probably include a creation story and not the story of migration across a land bridge.

Take the Gwawaenuk (gwa wa ā nook) creationism story for example. The first ancestor of the Gwawaenuk Tribe of the west coast of British Columbia is a Thunderbird. The Thunderbird is a supernatural creature who can fly through the heavens. One day, at the beginning of time, the Thunderbird landed on top of Mt. Stevens in the Broughton Archipelago at the northern tip of Vancouver Island. Upon landing on Mt. Stevens, the Thunderbird transformed into human form, becoming the first ancestor of the Gwawaenuk people. This act signals the creation of the Gwawaenuk people as well as defining the territory which the Gwawaenuk people would use and protect.

Now, the idea of a Thunderbird landing on a mountain and transforming into a human being may sound unusual and a little silly, but to a Gwawaenuk person it doesn't sound any more unusual or silly than a virgin birth, or a person walking on water, coming back from the dead, or parting the Red Sea. It is what they believe—and if we want to be effective, we cannot undermine their core religious and spiritual beliefs.

Indigenous Peoples across Canada each have their own creation belief that is told in the form of a story of their ancestors. The Iroquois creation story often includes elements of the earth being formed on the turtle's back, and hence the expression Turtle Island.

The Inuit creation belief often includes a story of the world being made by Raven, a man with a raven's beak. Raven drew the ground up from the water and fixed it into place.

> "The Great Land of the Inuit is the sea, the earth, the moon, the sun, the sky and stars. The land and the sea have no boundaries. It is not mine and it is not yours. The Supreme Being put it there and did not give it to us. We were put there to be part of it and share it with other beings, the birds, fish, animals and plants."[1]

Wheels, Written Languages, and the Primitive Cultures

Another widely held belief about the Indigenous Peoples who populated the Americas at the time of Christopher Columbus is that they were primitive cultures living in primitive conditions. Dictionaries define "primitive" as being of an early age, crude, simple, little evolved, unsophisticated, or produced by a people or culture that is non-industrial, often non-literate, and tribal. These definitions of primitive suggest that Indigenous Peoples lived in undeveloped, simple, and unsophisticated societies at the time of Columbus' arrival to the Americas.

More specifically, it has been suggested that cultures without wheels or written languages, were often considered primitive. This is another example of an ethnocentric view of primitive cultures. In what has become Canada, the utility of a wheel was significantly limited by topography. In some parts of Canada, it would have been almost impossible to roll one wheel by itself let alone two side by side on an axle. The Indigenous Peoples had other methods of travel that better suited the topography, such as birch bark or cedar dugout canoes or kayaks—efficient methods of travel that were quickly adopted by the European settlers.

While many of the Indigenous Peoples of North America relied on oral histories instead of a written language, Indigenous Peoples were recording historical events in the form of pictographs in various materials. The Maya and Inca were recording history in stone while some of the plains peoples were recording historical events on buffalo hides and some of the Indigenous Peoples west of the Canadian Rockies were recording historical events in pictographs.

Many Indigenous communities in North America lived in societies reliant upon oral histories. They passed their history to future generations through stories, songs, and oral communications. These histories have been considered accurate enough that the Supreme Court of Canada in 1997 ruled that oral testimony and oral history are admissible as evidence in a court of law where the history can be corroborated.[2] This substantiates the weight put on the spoken word by Indigenous Peoples. It cannot be emphasized enough that extra attention be paid to verbal commitments made to Indigenous Peoples due to their historical reliance upon oral communications.

All Indigenous Peoples were Nomadic

There has been a long-held idea that all Indigenous Peoples were nomadic peoples living in primitive conditions roaming the land searching for their next meal. There is a great deal of archaeological evidence to suggest that while some Indigenous Peoples were nomadic, a great number were not. For example, midden sites in coastal British Columbia date back thousands of years. A midden site is where Indigenous People heaped their clam shells after consumption. Archaeologists use these midden sites to count the layers of clam shells, like rings on a tree, to see how long and how many people lived in an area. This is a clear indication that some Indigenous Peoples were stationary, and if they did move, it was to go from a summer house site to a winter house site. In the Fraser Valley, one of the popular Sto:lo First Nation sites at Xá:ytem[3] is dated at about 9000 years ago—providing evidence of continued occupation of one site for a significant length of time.

There were other Indigenous Peoples who did move around throughout the year; fishing in one place in the summer and hunting in another in the winter, but it was always within a traditional territory. Sometimes those territories were shared with other communities; for example, the Cree, Assiniboine, and Ojibway share a similar history and cultural traditions due to their use of overlapping territory for hunting and gathering of food. The distinction here is they moved around within their territory utilizing different parts of it at different times of the year, as opposed to blindly following migratory animals.

They had Primitive Engineering Knowledge

When people think of Indigenous Peoples engineering abilities prior to European explorers, they probably conjure up images of the iconic tipi or inukshuk—perhaps not much more than that. In fact, Indigenous Peoples were building super-structures, long houses (also known as big houses), or igloos. In addition, some Indigenous Peoples were creating calendars and vulcanizing rubber.

The Maya of Mexico's Yucatan Peninsula are a great example of the engineering abilities of Indigenous Peoples on the Americas prior to contact. The Maya developed highly sophisticated urban cultures and the supporting infrastructure. They used huge stone blocks to erect magnificent temples and monuments. "Modern" science continues to struggle to understand how the temples and monuments were built and how those massive blocks were moved from their original location to be placed 72 metres above ground level.

Trade networks and communications

There is a commonly held belief that Indigenous Peoples were living in isolated communities, limited by topography. This isolation was thought to prohibit Indigenous Peoples from moving large numbers of goods, services, or ideas. In fact, prior to contact by European explorers, Indigenous Peoples had extensive trade networks in place allowing for the movement of people and goods over hundreds of miles at a time. On the west coast of what we now know as North America, these trade networks extended from Alaska to California and even into other provinces and states.

The trade networks were made possible by water-way travel across the ocean, rivers, and lakes, and by the use of a common trade language called Chinook. Chinook Jargon allowed travellers and traders from very diverse cultures with completely different languages the ability to communicate with each other, thereby promoting the exchange of goods, services, and ideas over vast areas of country.

Aquaculture to Agriculture and Food Preservation

Pre-contact fishing to Indigenous Peoples of the northwest coast of North America did not mean solely relying on nature to provide an abundant supply of fish and shellfish. Indigenous Peoples on the northwest coast were involved in aquaculture methods to enhance the production of shellfish returns. They deliberately placed stones in formations just below the low tide water line that would allow shellfish, such as clams, to grow more abundantly in those areas.

In many other parts of the Americas, Indigenous Peoples were practicing agricultural techniques to enhance the abundance of food grown in their natural habitat. The Iroquois were involved in slash and burn farming of maize, squash, and beans, while the Indigenous people of the Caribbean were farming using the process of conucos (heaping soil to prevent erosion) and the penning of animals for later use.[4]

Such aquaculture and agricultural practices created an excess of supply of food that required Indigenous Peoples to develop techniques of food preservation and storage for the off season. These storage techniques included pemmican of the Cree and Blackfoot, the wind dried salmon, and smoked and salted fish of the west coast Nations, and the dried roots of the Indigenous people of the Caribbean. The drying and storage techniques extended the supply of food, thereby supporting large populations of people with relative ease. In the highest altitudes of the Andes, the Incas used overnight freezing temperatures to freeze dry food—potatoes, in particular. The Incas transported the potatoes into the mountains, covered them with a cloth, leaving them to freeze overnight, and then in the morning, the villagers would walk on the cloths, squishing out the moisture, thereby creating freeze-dried potatoes.

Anthropological evidence has determined that in British Columbia, some Indigenous Peoples living near salmon-bearing rivers were found to work just over two months a year gathering enough food and other supplies necessary to comfortably survive the rest of the year.[5] This left significant amounts of time available to develop sophisticated cultures and governance systems.

They had Primitive Models of Governance

Indigenous Peoples models of governance varied across North America in terms of levels of sophistication. Some were fairly informal governing structures while others were very sophisticated, again rivalling any in the world at the time of contact. What is it that drives governance structures and the level of sophistication of governance? People.

WORKING EFFECTIVELY TIP:
Many early Indigenous cultures rivalled other cultures in the world. Therefore, don't insist that what you have to offer is a better idea than what Indigenous Peoples have or had.

In areas where Indigenous Peoples moved around a wide territory in small groups, some could say that the governance structure would be less sophisticated and more informal. In such circumstances, there would be little requirement for a sophisticated and formal decision-making structure. There were likely more opportunities for everyone to play some kind of role in the governing process in these smaller groups.

On the other hand, whenever large populations of people live in small geographical areas, more sophisticated models of governance are necessary to provide a formal decision-making structure. The governing structure developed by the Six Nations people[6] of the northeastern region of North America is the oldest living participatory democracy on earth. When Benjamin Franklin and Thomas Jefferson were drafting the representative democracy contained in the Constitution of the United States, they drew inspiration from the Six Nations' participatory democracy.

1492—Arrival in the "New World"

The arrival of European explorers in the Americas began the introduction of European culture to the New World. The enormity of the impact on the Indigenous Peoples of the Americas created by the arrival of Christopher Columbus in 1492 (and by the waves of Europeans who soon followed him) is beyond comprehension.

There is still a widely held perception that the Americas were essentially empty when Columbus arrived in 1492 to "discover" the New World—except for a few primitive savages in the wilderness. The numbers indicate that the "New World" was anything but vacant: "by 1492 there were approximately 100 million Native Americans—a fifth, more or less, of the human race."[7]

From the perspective of that fifth of the world's population, it is really hard to understand how you can "discover" a place that is already home to 100 million people. Further, to them, it was not a "new" world, but a world as old as time itself, going back to creation. It is for this reason that we describe Christopher Columbus' arrival to the Americas and not his discovery of the Americas.

Contact happened at different times and in different places for North and South American Indigenous People. The extent and impact of contact also varied. For some, contact came on strong and with catastrophic effect. For others, contact happened sporadically and under circumstances that allowed for adaptation and even some success. It is interesting to note the view held by R.E. Gosnell, the first British Columbia Legislative Librarian and Provincial Archivist at the turn of the twentieth century, regarding B.C.'s coastal Indigenous Peoples:[8]

"… One thing which has tended largely to their benefit is their position of independence. With the exception of being in a general way under the aegis of the Indian Department they receive no special favours such as are accorded to the Treaty Indians—no annuities or financial assistance. They are obliged to maintain themselves by hunting, fishing, trade and labour, the opportunities for which are always at hand. Game is abundant, the sea and rivers teem with fish; during the canning season, they are largely employed at good wages, and at various seasons earn money lumbering, on the farm, and in other capacities. They are, as compared with their eastern brethren, industrious, and are usually well supplied with ready cash for all their necessities. Such a thing as famine or starvation among our Indians is extremely rare, if, indeed, it ever occurs. Their trade is highly esteemed by traders, and is as a rule a fairly lucrative one…"

In eastern Canada, contact began around 1100, in what is now called Newfoundland. The Beothuk People of Newfoundland were the first Indigenous People to come into contact with Europeans—contact that tragically set the stage for their eventual extinction. The Beothuk population, over its 2,000 year history, was never robust—historians estimate the number to be between 500 and 1,000 at the time of European contact in 1497 when John Cabot arrived on the island. Fewer than 350 years later, the Beothuk were extinct.

The first wave of Europeans who arrived to harvest the bounties of the sea did not establish settlements, but rather had seasonal camps, returning to their homelands before winter. The Beothuk were able to co-exist with this seasonal presence and appear to have had a mutually beneficial relationship based on a system of "silent" bartering in which one group would leave items of interest to the other group at a customary spot and vice versa.

Peaceful, seasonal co-existence came to an abrupt end in the 17th century when Europeans established settlements on the coast in the traditional gathering points of the Beothuk, which had an immediate and profound impact on the Beothuk. Their nomadic lifestyle was dramatically disrupted as they were increasingly cut off from the sea, a vital food source. As the European population increased, so did their hunting and trapping of fur-bearing animals. This further impacted the

Beothuk. The migratory routes of the caribou were disrupted and the herds were severely over-hunted. The Beothuk retaliated and violent confrontations erupted as they struggled to defend their lifestyle and very existence; but the Beothuk were using arrows, which were no match for firearms, so these confrontations unfailingly resulted in high death rates for the Beothuk.

Viewed by some settlers as savages, less than human, and as a threat to the safety of their settlements, the Beothuk were systematically hunted with the intent to eradicate all of them from the island. This period of viciousness coincided with a series of extreme winters, which further decimated the Beothuk. They slowly starved as their traditional hunting and fishing grounds were taken from them; they struggled to maintain their deer fences and hunting practices, but—due to their diminished numbers—they were unable to do so. Those other European introductions—tuberculosis, smallpox, measles—further devastated the population.

Government leaders grew concerned about the rumours they heard regarding the plight of the Beothuk. In a display of extreme naivety, they offered a reward for the capture of live Beothuks—the intent being that the captives would be well treated, would learn to view the Europeans as benign, and, once convinced of this view, would be allowed to return to their families and spread the word; the Beothuks would learn to trust them and would move closer to the European settlements where they could receive help. There were two fundamental problems with this plan: Beothuk beliefs stipulated that if they made peace with the Europeans, their spirits would be denied access to Spirit Island; and the offer of the reward actually accelerated the demise of the Beothuks as the settlers took it to mean captive at any cost.

What little traditional knowledge there is on record is due to the offerings of Shanawdithit, the last remaining Beothuk who was found, starving, along with two other women in the spring of 1823. The other two women died shortly thereafter of tuberculosis, but Shanawdithit survived. She was placed in the care of the William Cormack, a merchant philanthropist. Cormack encouraged Shanawdithit to record her knowledge of her people, her culture, and language. Shanawdithit died of tuberculosis on June 6, 1829. The drawings of this brave young woman, the last Beothuk on earth, form the foundation of our scanty knowledge of a people lost forever.

First Claim to Canada

The first claim to land in Canada came from John Cabot in 1497. He was sent by the King of England to establish a fur trade, but was unable to make contact with Indigenous People and left the East coast without the fur trade—but with stories of abundant fish.

France didn't claim territory in Canada until 37 years after the English, when Jacques Cartier reached the Gaspé Peninsula. He returned to France shortly thereafter. only to return to Canada the following year. During this second trip he sailed up the St. Lawrence River to Stadacona (now Québec City) and to Hochelaga (now Montréal).

The first permanent European settlement in eastern Canada was founded by Samuel de Champlain of France. Trade between the French and the Mi'kmaq for goods and beaver furs fuelled future settlements up the St. Lawrence River and spread westward as the demand for beaver furs increased in Europe.

The English and French settlements in Canada extended their longstanding intermittent European conflict in a bitter struggle for control of New World peoples, territories, and trade. Indigenous Peoples in the area found themselves aligning with either side of these conflicts and became invaluable to the settlers. France aligned itself with the Huron which resulted in the Huron's enemies, the Iroquois, aligning with the British.

The collapse of France's power in the Seven Years' War (the world's first global conflict, lasting from 1756–63) saw its Indigenous Allies grow concerned in Canada. England, looking for stability, passed *The Royal Proclamation of 1763* providing all Indigenous People with the assurance that they would not be disturbed in their territories beyond the settled colonies.[9]

Support of all Indigenous People, previous allies and enemies, to the British military became invaluable in the War of 1812. Without Indigenous support, Britain was woefully outnumbered by the American military as it invaded Canada. After numerous losses in battle, the Americans retreated in 1814. This provided Canada with a newfound sense of nationhood.

By contrast, the primary focus of the eighteenth century Spanish and Russian explorers who travelled up and down the west coast of North America was less invasive. Trading for furs and searching for an inland passage across the continent to the Atlantic mattered more than conquest.

In 1778, Captain James Cook of Britain and his storm-battered crew became the first non-Indigenous people to land on the west coast of Vancouver Island, as well as chart the region. By the 1790s, the Spanish had claimed the west coast from

Mexico to Vancouver Island and the Russians had made an overlapping claim for control of the Pacific coast from Alaska to San Francisco. Neither nation had made much headway in establishing sovereignty.[10]

By 1849, Britain had declared Vancouver Island as a Colony of the Empire, following in 1858 with the formation of the Colony of British Columbia. In general, European contact came much later and with far less initial impact in western Canada than in what became Canada's eastern provinces. Non-Indigenous people didn't begin to settle in British Columbia in significant numbers until after 1850.

Disease, Death, and Depopulation

Throughout the Americas, Indigenous contact with Europeans was soon followed with drastic declines in Indigenous population. With no natural immunity to diseases introduced by the Europeans, Indigenous Peoples were decimated by waves of epidemics of smallpox, tuberculosis, scarlet fever, influenza, and measles. The Indigenous population at the time of contact in what is now known as Canada has been estimated at 500,000.[11] During 200-300 years of contact European introduced diseases had caused that number to fall quite.

Don't conquered peoples only have the rights we give them?

I must confess that when I was younger I, like many Canadians, had the idea that Indigenous Peoples in Canada were essentially conquered as part of the colonization process of Canada. I'm pretty sure I based my ideas, as did others, on the old John Wayne-type movies coming out of Hollywood.

When I was a small boy who watched way too many of these movies, we moved from Vancouver Island to a small First Nation community where my dad had recently begun working for the local band office. The first day in our new home I was outside playing in the puddles, as all children do, when a couple stopped at our house and began to get out of the car. This couple had long hair, just like the Indians in the John Wayne movies. I ran into the house, slamming the door in the faces of the couple, yelling "Mom, there's Indians out there!" My parents and their visitors—my relatives—laughed uproariously for a long time.

I know I embarrassed my parents that day because there have been many occasions for them to remind me of this story. I would, of course, learn much later that there was little in the way of "Indian wars" in Canada as portrayed in the old John Wayne movies that reflected more of an American experience.

The *Royal Proclamation* of 1763 and Pre-Confederation Treaties

In Canada, the relationship between the Crown and Indigenous Peoples has been driven primarily by the *Royal Proclamation* of October 1763. Of particular importance is the passage below which states:

> "It is just and reasonable and essential to our Interest, and the Security of our Colonies, that the several Nations or Tribes of Indians with whom We are connected, and who live under our Protection, should not be molested or disturbed in the Possession of such parts of our Dominions and Territories as not having been ceded to or purchased by Us, are reserved to them, or any of them, as their Hunting Grounds... any Lands whatever, which, not having been ceded to or purchased by Us as aforesaid, are reserved to the said Indians, or any of them...
>
> And We do hereby strictly forbid, on Pain of our Displeasure, all our loving Subjects from making any Purchases or Settlements whatever, or taking Possession of any of the Lands above reserved, without our especial leave and Licence for that Purpose first obtained.
>
> And We do further strictly enjoin and require all Persons whatever who have either wilfully or inadvertently seated themselves upon any Lands within the Countries above described or upon any other Lands which, not having been ceded to or purchased by Us, are still reserved to the said Indians as aforesaid, forthwith to remove themselves from such Settlements."

This section of the *Royal Proclamation* of 1763 is important because it refers to Nations or Tribes of Indians, thereby recognizing the Indigenous Peoples as owners of the lands that the Europeans were using and occupying, and sets out what today are sometimes called "special" hunting rights. The idea of "Nations" comes from King George III and his colonial government and confirms the international convention of the day that colonizing countries that reached inhabited lands were to conduct government business with the inhabitants on a Nation-to-Nation basis and treat those inhabitants as owners of the lands.

Even today, under the British Columbia Treaty Commission and the federal comprehensive claims policy, Indigenous Peoples have been approached by governments on a Nation-to-Nation basis. Any efforts to treat Indigenous Peoples as anything less will likely be met with resistance by the Indigenous communities. There is an expectation within the Indigenous community that they be treated as a nation as provided by the *Royal Proclamation*. As evidence of this expectation, many bands changed their band names to a First Nation name—for example, the Moose Factory Band of Indians changed to the Moose Cree First Nations.

The *Royal Proclamation* is regarded as early and powerful evidence of the recognition of Aboriginal rights in Canadian law, paving the way for the Supreme Court of Canada to rule in a series of cases beginning with *Calder*[12] that Aboriginal title both pre-existed and survived colonial occupation. In that light, these are the Proclamation's keywords: **"… any lands that had not been ceded to or purchased by Us as aforesaid, are reserved to the said Indians."** (emphasis added)

In addition to the recognition of Aboriginal title, the *Royal Proclamation* also recognizes Aboriginal rights to harvest resources from their territories. This principle is acknowledged [in that the Aboriginal lands are "… **reserved to them, or any of them, as their Hunting Grounds."**

Many of Canada's modern day landmark court cases have drawn their legal principles from principles in the *Proclamation,* but why would there be a need for the *Royal Proclamation* when King George III was in charge of one of the most powerful nations at that time with technological and military advantage? The answer to his approach lay in the political and military environment of the time. On both the Atlantic and Pacific fronts, early developments promised a more mutually beneficial approach to European-Indigenous engagement than what ultimately transpired. In the initial years of contact, the balance of power was still in flux. Because the European technological and military advantage was ultimately so overwhelming, it is easy to forget how organized, sophisticated, and powerful many Indigenous Nations were in those days. The Europeans desperately needed them as trading partners, wilderness-survival tutors, and military allies. The *Royal Proclamation* was King George III's way of building and maintaining additional loyalties from Indigenous Peoples, thereby encouraging Indigenous support of England, and reducing loyalties to the French, Spanish, and Russians—key trading and military partners. This also gave him the support he needed to prevail over these competing colonizing and trading interests.

Pragmatism to Paternalism

During the half-century directly following the *Royal Proclamation*, the colonial governments of North America signed a number of peace and land treaties with Indigenous Peoples in order to retain them as allies and to obtain land for settlement and resource development. Many of these treaties were in fact blank sheets of paper because, for example, British Columbia Governor James Douglas was waiting for the wording of the treaty to arrive by ship from New Zealand. The British Crown was entering into treaties around the world and was looking to keep the wording consistent. There are many similarities between the Douglas Treaties and the New Zealand Treaty of Waitangi.

During this period of heightened treaty signing, the balance of power began to shift as the British consolidated their control. The pragmatism that had prompted the British Crown to protect Aboriginal interests in the *Royal Proclamation* gave way to British paternalism, a policy of assimilation, and the attitude that Aboriginal Peoples were British subjects—not equal, independent nations.

Niagara Treaty, 1764
Fort Stanwix Treaty, 1768
Treaty of Paris, 1783
Upper Canada Treaties, 1764–1836
The Jay Treaty, 1794
The Selkirk Treaty, 1817
Rescinding the Niagara Treaty, 1836
Bond Head Treaties, 1836
Province of Canada Treaties, 1850–1862
The Douglas Treaties, 1850–1854

The Métis Nation: A Battered but Unbroken People

During the 1600s, France began establishing settlements along the St. Lawrence River to advance its fur trade interests. The prevailing "seigneurial" landholding system was a legacy of the feudal age: rigid and restrictive. So, enterprising Frenchmen—soon to be known as "coureurs des bois" (runners in the woods)—sought to improve their prospects by venturing into the wilderness, despite restrictions imposed on them by King Louis XIV. The coureurs des bois began establishing homes for themselves within, or beside, Indian communities, marrying Indian women, and starting families. The birth of their children marked the birth of the Métis Nation.[13]

The word "Métis" comes from the Latin "miscere" meaning "to mix" and is used generally to describe European men and Indigenous women who had children together. It is understood by Métis people today that the intermarriage of their ancestors involved more than just the blending of races and cultures—it was an evolution that culminated in the birth of a new Indigenous Nation with its own language, called Michif. The Métis people had their own food, clothing, history, body politic, and flag. There is a national definition of Métis—it means a person who self-identifies as Métis, is of historic Métis Nation ancestry, is distinct from other Indigenous Peoples, and is accepted or recognized by the Métis Nation.

The Métis people played an important role in the history of Canada. They often acted as middlemen between Europeans and Indigenous Peoples, encouraging trade and commerce, and mediating disputes. Also, and perhaps of more significance, their legendary struggles for independence in the Red River Rebellion of 1869-70 and the North-West Rebellion of 1885 have inspired other Indigenous Peoples in their quests for greater autonomy.

The Red River Settlement

In 1801, a group of Métis settled at the intersection of the Red and Assiniboine Rivers, where Winnipeg stands today. They were referred to as "Freemen" because they were bound by neither Indian nor Fur Trade company law. They set up narrow river lots similar to the seigneurial lots created earlier along the St. Lawrence and established the Red River Settlement.

In 1811, the Hudson's Bay Company granted 116,000 square miles of land in the fertile Red River Valley to Lord Selkirk. Efforts by the settlers of this land to restrict Indigenous hunting and trading practices led to conflict with the Métis. In 1816, Cuthbert Grant, Jr., led the Métis to victory at the battle of Seven Oaks.

By the 1840s, the Red River Settlement's population had swelled to 5,800 Métis and 1,600 non-Indigenous Peoples. The Hudson's Bay Company was uneasy about the threat to its fur trading monopoly posed by the Settlement's burgeoning commercial activity. In 1849, the Company's directors persuaded the North-West Police to charge four Métis men with "smuggling" furs. Louis Riel, Sr., and approximately 300 other Métis surrounded the courthouse and heard the court pronounce the traders "Guilty"—but they were released without punishment. The Métis interpreted this ambiguous result as an acquittal and concluded that no one could be penalized for trading furs. The case is significant because it sparked the perception that the fur-trading monopoly of the Hudson's Bay Company had been broken, fanning the commercial aspirations of the Métis.

The new Dominion of Canada recognized the urgent need to consolidate its western and southern borders against the threat of American expansion, and the Hudson's Bay Company saw that it was unable to control the Red River Settlers. In 1869, one of the key events in Canadian history quietly unfolded—the Dominion of Canada purchased the vast territory of Rupert's Land[14] from the Hudson's Bay Company for the sum of 300,000 English pounds. By that time, an estimated 11,000 people lived in the Red River Settlement within the boundaries of Rupert's Land, yet no one from the Settlement was informed about the sale.

Upon learning of the sale, the Métis rebelled under the leadership of Louis Riel, Jr. After a period of brilliant military and political success, Riel allowed his new Provisional Government to execute Thomas Scott, an unrepentant Orangeman from

Ontario who had been charged with bearing arms against the new state. Scott's instant martyrdom following his execution led to Riel's undoing.

In 1871, the Parliament of Canada passed the *Manitoba Act* providing for the acceptance of the Red River Settlement and surrounding territories into Canada as a full-fledged province, and calling for the dispatch of twelve hundred soldiers to "protect" the settlements. After more than three months of hard marching through the bush and muskeg, the troops from Ontario arrived to arrest Riel. He fled to the United States, where he remained in exile for more than a decade.[15]

Louis Riel, Jr., and the Northwest Rebellion of 1885

The Northwest Rebellion of 1885 began with Louis Riel, Jr., returning from the United States with his wife, two small children, and a few supporters to seize the church at Batoche, Saskatchewan, declaring, "Rome has fallen." Riel formed the Provisional Government of the Saskatchewan and sent 400 men into action under the leadership of Gabriel Dumont, a great Métis buffalo hunter and master of guerrilla strategy. Among the demands of the Métis were local control of lands, responsible government, parliamentary representation, and confirmation of their land title in accordance with the river lot system survey. While the rebels won a few legendary guerrilla battles (i.e., at Duck Lake and Fish Creek), ultimately Riel and Dumont lacked the resources needed to prevail.

In the end, Riel saw at least one of his visions fulfilled. Just before crossing into Canada from the United States on his way to Batoche, he confided to a priest: "I see a gallows on top of that hill, and I am swinging from it." He was convicted of treason and hanged on November 16, 1885.

Riel's vision and determination influences Métis people of today to continue to thrive and grow in Canada.

B. 1867—NATIONS TO WARDS

The *British North America Act*

Canada officially became a country in 1867 with the passage of the *British North America Act*.[1] Pursuant to section 91(24) of the *Act*, the federal government was given authority to make laws about "Indians and lands reserved for the Indians."[2] The *Act* marked a significant change in Indian policy from a Nation-to-Nation relationship to one of wards of the Crown and a policy of forced cultural assimilation. The *Act* introduced an era that would have a lasting impact on the Canadian state.

The *Indian Act*

Many laws affecting Indigenous Peoples were combined in 1876 to become the *Indian Act*. The *Indian Act* gave Canada a coordinated approach to Indian policy rather than the pre-Confederation piecemeal approach, addressing three main areas of legislation: **land, membership,** and **local government**.

The Indian agent, acting under the authority of the *Indian Act*, played a key role in the distribution of land, replacing traditional names for "easier" identification, and altering traditional and hereditary forms of government.

Land —The Indian agent drew the boundaries on parcels of land that were set aside for the use and benefit of Indigenous Peoples. These lands became known as reserve lands as opposed to reservations, which is the American term.

Membership—In order to account for the numbers of people living on the reserves, the Indian agent would arrive in a community with a pen and piece of paper and ask for names. This is how the process would have unfolded: I would be asked my name, I would say "k'acksum, nakwala," and they would write down "Bob Joseph." At this point I became a Status Indian because my name appeared on a band list. That listing of names would then become the band. The Indian agents on the west coast of Canada often used English and biblical names, repeating them as often as they wished. I am often asked if I am related to the Josephs from the Squamish First Nation, to which I usually reply "No, but I'm sure we had the same Indian agent."

Local Government—The Indian agents also decided that if assimilation were to succeed, then a uniform form of government was required. Communities were forced to abandon the hereditary chieftainship or other forms of traditional leadership and governance system and to elect a chief and council. While the hereditary system lost to the local governance authority, it remained part of the culture. It is why it is possible to meet band chiefs and hereditary chiefs in the same meeting.

The *Indian Act* has been a lightning rod for criticism and controversy over the years, widely attacked by Indigenous Peoples and communities for its regressive and paternalistic excesses. For example, Indians living on reserves don't own the land they live on; assets on reserve are not subject to seizure under legal process, making it extremely difficult to borrow money to purchase assets; and matrimonial property laws don't apply to assets on reserve. Additionally, it is also widely attacked by non-Indigenous people and politicians as being too paternalistic and creating an unjust system with excessive costs that are considered uneconomical.

Assimilation

As mentioned, prior to 1867, Aboriginal Peoples were considered Nations as confirmed by the *Royal Proclamation*. Even after the introduction of the *Indian Act* in 1867 we see the continued negotiation of treaties on a Nation-to-Nation basis moving forward with a number of post-Confederation treaties. The Numbered Treaties—or Post-Confederation Treaties—were signed between 1871 and 1921, and granted the federal government large tracts of land throughout the Prairies, northern Canada, and north western Ontario for white settlement and industrial use. In exchange for their land, Indigenous Peoples were promised cash, blankets, tools, farming supplies, and so on.

This effort to continue negotiating treaties on a Nation-to-Nation basis needs to be contrasted with the aggressive efforts of assimilation that ultimately flow out of the British North America Act.

By 1880, the government of Canada had decided to apply its broad *Indian Act* powers to the strategic goal of assimilating Indigenous Peoples into the mainstream of Canadian society. On May 5, 1880, Sir John A. Macdonald stood in the House of Commons to announce that his government's Indian policy was:

> "... to wean them by slow degrees, from their nomadic habits, which have almost become an instinct, and by slow degrees absorb them or settle them on the land. Meantime they must be fairly protected."

A number of specific measures were systematically deployed to give effect to this assimilation policy, some of which are outlined below.

Permits

Permit to leave reserve

During the heyday of assimilation, First Nations required a permit from the Indian agent in order to leave the boundary of his or her reserve; they also were not allowed in public places, such as cafes or pool rooms.

Following the Red River Rebellion and Northwest Rebellion, immigration to Saskatchewan slowed down, which interrupted the plans of Prime Minister John A. Macdonald to develop the agricultural potential of the West. A means of controlling the movements of the "rebel Indians" was deemed necessary to ensure farmers they were safe, and to prevent future collaborations between reserves that might result in another uprising.

> "In 1885, the Department of Indian Affairs instituted a pass system. No outsider could come onto a reserve to do business with an Aboriginal resident without permission from the Indian agent. In many places, the directives were interpreted to mean that no Aboriginal person could leave the reserve without permission from the Indian agent. Reserves were beginning to resemble prisons."[3]

The "pass system" was devised in which Indian agents were supplied with books of passes, or permits to leave. The passes stipulated the time the individual was allowed to be off-reserve as well as the purpose of the time away, and whether or not the individual was allowed to carry a gun. The pass system was initially applied to rebel Indians, but later expanded for all First Nations.

In order to obtain a pass, individuals would often have to travel many days by foot to the Agent's house, not knowing if he would be there when they arrived. If the Agent were away, they would either camp and wait, or return home. If the need to leave the reserve was pressing, such as to sell market-ready produce, the delay resulted in produce that rotted.

The pass system was also a means of maintaining a separation between First Nations and the European farmers—which seems illogical in the context of that era of assimilation—it's hard to achieve assimilation if the target population is isolated on reserves. The pass system restricted access to local towns in order to prevent First Nations farmers from wasting their time when they should be tending their crops... crops they were restricted from selling. The pass system additionally enabled the government to attempt to quash potlatches, the Sun Dance, and other cultural practices.

Parents required passes to visit their children interned at residential schools. Controlling parents' access to their children aided and abetted the government's policy of removing "the Indian from the child." Parents were given a limited number of passes to visit their children during the school year. If a child was ill, and if the parents were informed, then they might be given additional passes to visit.

The pass system was created in 1885, enforced into the 1940s, and repealed in 1951.

Permit to sell

Under the *Indian Act,* the reserve system was created which effectively removed First Nations from their traditional territories and lifestyles in some cases and positioned the government to attempt to dispossess them of their culture and identity. Once First Nations were moved onto the reserves, into European style houses, given European names, and entered into the registry, it became much easier to administer policies.

Agriculture was chosen as the path for First Nations to follow towards "civilization." Hayter Reed, Deputy Superintendent General of Indian Affairs from 1893-1897, stated "agriculture was the great panacea of what was perceived to be the ills of Canada's Indians."[4] This is despite the fact that many reserves were located in areas that were unsuitable for agriculture. Government agencies later used the low success rate of First Nation farmers as reason to reduce the size of reserves.

Indian agents and farm instructors worked with the First Nations to teach them how to farm, although raising crops such as corn or rice was not new to some cultures. In Saskatchewan in particular, some of the First Nation farmers were very successful and grew crops and produce as good or better than that produced by the settlers. They formed collectives to share the costs of new equipment and labour.

"At Duck Lake in 1891, six or seven Indians together purchased a self-binder with the approval of the farm instructor. The implement dealer had to acquire the consent of the agent, who was ordered by Inspector McGibbon to object to the sale. No sale or delivery took place."[5]

The unexpected farming success quickly became a problem, and new policies were developed to protect the market share for the settlers. *An Act to Amend "The Indian Act, 1880,"* prohibited the sale of agricultural products grown on reserves in the Territories, Manitoba, or the District of Keewatin—except in accordance with government regulations. In other words, First Nation farmers had to have a permit to sell cattle, grain, a load of hay, or produce; additionally, they required a permit to buy groceries and clothes. To solidify the effectiveness of the permit system, settlers were prohibited from purchasing goods and services from First Nation farmers.

Penalty for buying from Indians contrary to such regulations.

2. Any person who buys or otherwise acquires from any such Indian, or band, or irregular band of Indians, contrary to any provisions or regulations made by the Governor in Council under this Act, is guilty of an offence, and is punishable, upon summary conviction, by fine, not exceeding one hundred dollars, or by imprisonment for a period not exceeding three months, in any place of confinement other than a penitentiary, or by both fine and imprisonment."[6]

The permit system ensured that First Nations were only able to attain a subsistence level of farming. It also limited interaction between First Nation farmers and the non-First Nations in the area.

In the 1951 *Act*, the permit system was extended to cover all First Nations but its enforcement gradually disappeared.

Women's Status—Discrimination via Bill C-31, Bill C-3

Indian Act policies subjected generations of Indigenous women and their children to a legacy of discrimination when it was first enacted in 1876, and continues to do so today despite amendments. Federal law in the late 1800s defined a status Indian solely on the basis of paternal lineage—an Indian was a male Indian, the wife of a male Indian, or the child of a male Indian—which continues to be a quagmire of discrimination and disrespect towards women. While there have been numerous amendments to the *Act*, Indian status continues to be transmitted by male Indians, never by female Indians.

From 1869 until 1985 (116 years), if an Indian woman married a non-Indian man, she and the children of the marriage were denied Indian status. In 1985, the *Indian Act* was amended by the passage of Bill C-31 to remove discrimination against women, to be consistent with section 15 of the *Canadian Charter of Rights and Freedoms,*[7] included in the 1982 amendment of the Constitution. Coming into effect on April 17, 1985, Section 15 provided that "every individual is equal before and under the law and has the right to the equal protection and benefit of the law without discrimination based on race, national or ethnic origin, colour, religion, sex, age, or mental or physical disability."

The *Report of the Royal Commission on Aboriginal Peoples* (1996) notes that strong concerns have been raised among Aboriginal people regarding Bill C-31's effective replacement of original *Indian Act* discriminatory provisions with new ones: For example, as noted in the Bill C-31 study summary report, "bands that control their own membership under the Act may now restrict eligibility for some of the rights and benefits that used to be automatic with status." Moreover, sex discrimination, supposedly wiped out by the 1985 amendments, remains. Thus, for example, in some families, Indian women who lost status through marrying out before 1985 can pass Indian status on to their children, but not to their children's children—the "second generation cut-off." However, their brothers, who may also have married out before 1985, can pass on status to their children for at least one more generation, even though the children of the sister and the brother all have one status Indian parent and one non-Indian parent."[8]

Amendments to Bill C-31 provided a process by which women could apply for reinstatement of their lost Indian status. While such an amendment looks good on paper, in some cases it proved to be extremely difficult for women to actually execute the process. The first of many hurdles was the then Department of Indian and Northern Affairs' (DIAND) documentation system—the numerous requests for additional information combined with the department's significant underestimation of the sheer volume of applicants and its inability to process the applications due to inadequate staffing levels frequently left the applicants in prolonged states of limbo. Besides the daunting magnitude of red tape involved, a more heartless aspect of the reinstatement process was the cost applicants were forced to bear as they travelled from sometimes very remote communities to centres that had DIAND offices, plus the costs for research and documentation fees. These costs and travel requirements simply put the dream of reinstatement, which opened the door to better health and education services for the women and their children, out of reach for many who were already financially marginalized due to their lack of status.

Bill C-3, introduced in March 2010, was supposed to be the remedy but actually continued the discrimination because the status reinstated is of inferior status. Grandchildren born before September 4, 1951 who trace their Aboriginal heritage through their maternal parentage are still denied status while those who trace their heritage through their paternal counterparts are not. In October 2016, Bill S-3 *An Act to amend the Indian Act* (elimination of sex-based inequities in registration) was introduced.

Potlatch Law

From 1884 to 1951, the *Indian Act* prohibited Indians from participating in the Potlatch and other similar cultural ceremonies across Canada. True assimilation could only be attained through the abolishment, by law, of all cultural practices. Hence, under the *Indian Act,* the Potlatch Law, which included other ceremonies such as the Sun Dance, came into effect in 1880.

Section 3 of *An Act Further to Amend The Indian Act, 1884* made the exercise of these practices a criminal offence:

"3. Every Indian or other person who engages in or assists in celebrating the Indian festival known as the 'Potlatch' or in the Indian dance known as the 'Tamanawas' is guilty of a misdemeanor, and shall be liable to imprisonment . . . and any Indian or other person who encourages . . . an Indian or Indians to get up such a festival or dance, or to celebrate the same . . . is guilty of a like offence . . ."

Potlatch ceremonies, depending upon the culture, could be held to celebrate the passing of names, titles, and responsibilities of one chief to the eldest heir; distribute wealth, establish rank; to mark the passing of a chief or the head of a house; or to celebrate weddings and births. Recognized as integral to the culture of coastal First Nations, the Potlatch was targeted with particular force. The government and missionaries viewed Potlatch ceremonies as excessive, wasteful, and barriers to assimilation.

"Clause three of the 1884 legislation endorsed the views of British Columbia agents and clergymen opposed to the celebration of the 'Potlatch' festival. These celebrations, which local officers and missionaries described as 'debauchery of the worst kind' were considered by the Deputy Superintendent-General to have 'pernicious effects' upon Indians. In a sense, this was a landmark amendment for it represented the first in a long series of attempts by Parliament to protect Indians from themselves as well as from unscrupulous 'whites.'"[9]

If the Potlatch, the cornerstone of the culture of coastal First Nations, could be eradicated, then the government and the missionaries would be free to swoop in and fill the cultural void with Christianity. On paper, this must have looked like a good idea; but in reality, all it did was drive the Potlatch underground. Resistance to losing the freedom to continue with traditions was severely underestimated.

One very famous example of an underground Potlatch took place at Christmas in 1921 in Alert Bay. 'Namgis Chief Dan Cranmer held a six day Potlatch to celebrate a wedding. The Potlatch was held on Village Island in an effort to keep the activities out from under the nose of the Indian agents and missionaries. Unfortunately, the celebration was detected, and under the Potlatch Law, 45 people were arrested and charged; 22 were jailed. Their crimes? Giving speeches, dancing, and gift-giving. An additional injustice was the loss of hundreds of priceless ceremonial items such as masks and regalia which were confiscated, and, over time, dispersed throughout the world through collectors and museums.

Potlatches continued to be held underground by a few determined communities, and the government eventually realized they were fighting a losing battle. Also, post-World War II, the Canadian public became aware of basic human rights and the appalling treatment of Aboriginal Peoples. In 1951, when the *Indian Act* was amended, the Potlatch Law was deleted. The first legal Potlatch was hosted by Chief Mungo Martin in Victoria in 1952.

In the 71 years of the Potlatch Law, almost an entire generation grew up deprived of the cultural fabric of their ancestors and countless thousands of irreplaceable ceremonial masks, robes, blankets, and other Potlatch items were lost forever to their People.

"This provision of the Indian Act was in place for close to 75 years and what that did was it prevented the passing down of our oral history. It prevented the passing down of our values. It meant an interruption of the respected forms of government that we used to have, and we did have forms of government be they oral, and not in writing before any of the Europeans came to this country. We had a system that worked for us. We respected each other. We had ways of dealing with disputes."[10]

Residential Schools

The beginning of what would become the Indian residential school system got its start in 1844 when the Bagot Commission of the United Province of Canada recommended training students in "… as many manual labour or Industrial schools as possible … In such schools … isolated from the influence of their parents, pupils would imperceptibly acquire the manners, habits and customs of civilized life."

WORKING EFFECTIVELY TIP:

Try not to come across to Indigenous Peoples as though you're from the government or that you are there to help. Instead, try a joint problem solving approach such as "I have lots to share, but I also know I have lots to learn."

In 1879, the Davin Report recommended residential schools based on the American model. Davin reported that the boarding school approach was the best answer because it "…took the Indian from the reserve and kept him in the constant circle of civilization, assured attendance, removed him from the retarding influence of his parents…" By 1931, 80 residential schools existed throughout Canada.

Requiring Indigenous children to participate in the public school system was seen as an important instrument of the assimilation policy, and compulsory attendance was incorporated into the *Indian Act* early in the twentieth century.

KAMLOOPS INDIAN RESIDENTIAL SCHOOL
KAMLOOPS, B. C.

November 18, 1948.

Dear Parents,

It will be your privilege this year to have your children spend Christmas at home with you. The holidays will extend from DECEMBER 18th. to JANUARY 3rd. This is a privilege which is being granted if you observe the following regulations of the Indian Department.

1. THE TRANSPORTATION TO THE HOME AND BACK TO THE SCHOOL MUST BE PAID BY THE PARENTS.

The parents must come themselves to get their own children. If they are unable to come they must send a letter to the Principal of the school stating that the parents of other children from the same Reserve may bring them home. The children will not be allowed to go home alone on the train or bus.

2. THE PARENTS MUST BRING THE CHILDREN BACK TO SCHOOL STRICTLY ON TIME.

If the children are not returned to school on time they will not be allowed to go home for Christmas next year.

I ask you to observe the above regulations in order that this privilege of going home for Christmas may be continued from year to year. It will be a joy for you to have your children with you for Christmas. It will be a joy also for your children and it will bring added cheer and happiness to your home.

Yours sincerely,

Rev. F. O'Grady, O.M.I.,
Principal.

Keep in mind that all of these measures were justified in part by officials as being measures designed to help Indigenous Peoples and bring them forward. The approach was, "We're from the government and we are here to help." In the grand scheme of things, Indigenous Peoples are not further ahead when you consider that prior to all the "help," they were self-determining, self-reliant, and self-governing.

Since it was widely assumed in the 1920s by non-Indigenous people that the Indian didn't have the "physical, mental, or moral get-up to enable him to compete," as one Indian Commissioner phrased it in a report to Ottawa, the only thing to do was to teach him a trade. Taking their grant money, the priests quickly set up residential schools—as far as possible from the bad influence of home, family, and friends. Indian children right across the country shared the common trauma of being dragged away from their homes and cast into strange places where they were beaten if caught speaking their own languages. Since the residential schools were all denominational, Christian indoctrination was the main focus: learning a trade came a poor second.

Not surprisingly, children ran away from the residential schools in droves. So many escaped that the RCMP were used to chase them down and haul them back into classes. The problem of escaping children got to the point where the government passed a law stating that Indian parents had no authority over their children while the children were in residential school.

The situation would have been enough of a nightmare for parents, grandparents, aunts, uncles, and children alike, even if it had not been coupled by the fact that non-Indigenous people had built such sub-standard buildings into which to herd a captive generation of young Indians that many of the children became sick and died. In 1914, Duncan Campbell Scott, former Deputy Superintendent General of Indian Affairs, confessed:

> "... the system was open to criticism. Insufficient care was exercised in the admission of children to the schools. The well-known predisposition of Indians to tuberculosis resulted in a very large percentage of deaths among the pupils. They were housed in buildings not carefully designed for school purposes, and these buildings became infected and dangerous to the **inmates. It is quite within the mark to say that fifty per cent of the children who passed through these schools did not live to benefit from the education which they had received therein.**" (emphasis added)

In 1951, the federal government began a four-decade long process of shutting down the schools; the last residential school for Indigenous children closed in

1996. Many of today's Indigenous People and leaders are survivors of the residential school program.

Although the last of the schools closed in 1996, the effect of the residential school system is intergenerational. Those children who were born after the closure of the schools were born to parents who likely attended and survived these schools. This generation of Indigenous children is learning their values, behaviours, attitudes, and beliefs from parents who felt abandoned by their own parents and communities, and abused by the church and state.

The well-known psychologist B.F. Skinner believed that we are all products of our environment. Children raised in a loving and supportive environment will more likely become loving and supportive adults and parents. Unfortunately, for the majority of the survivors of residential schools, they were not raised in such an environment and therefore are likely without the skills to provide a loving and supportive environment for their children. A lot of the social ills (i.e. alcoholism, violence, verbal and sexual abuse, and suicide) found in Indigenous communities have their roots firmly placed in the dark halls of the residential school system.

On June 11th, 2008, the Government of Canada issued a formal apology to the survivors of the residential schools. The apology was delivered by Prime Minister Stephen Harper in the House of Commons to representatives of the Indigenous Peoples, including the Indian, Inuit, and Métis Peoples. Among the many comments made by the Prime Minister, two in particular stood out that I think tell a large part of the story.

> "I stand before you today to offer an apology to former students of Indian residential schools. The treatment of children in these schools is a sad chapter in our history."

and

> "Today, we recognize that this policy of assimilation was wrong, has caused great harm, and has no place in our country."[11]

The Prime Ministerial apology, plus baseline compensation paid to survivors, and formation of the Truth and Reconciliation Commission (TRC) whose mandate is to help Canadians gain a common understanding of the full impact of Indian Residential Schools, represent many years of hard work by survivors' representatives to address this history. It is important to note that there is still much healing to do in Indigenous communities across the country and that individual survivors themselves will make a personal choice about whether to accept the apology or not.

The most recent development in the residential school saga was the declaration by the Truth and Reconciliation Commission that the schools were an attempt at cultural genocide and the more important and ongoing commitment to reconciliation. Be sure to check out the 94 recommendations of the TRC and find ways to work on them individually and organizationally.

Indigenous War Veterans

Indigenous People in Canada have fought on the front line of every major battle Canada has been involved in, and have done so with valour and distinction. It is estimated that 12,000[12] Indigenous People served in the First and Second World Wars, and the Korean War; an unknown number of Métis, Inuit, and non-status Indians also served. However, it was not until 1995, fifty years after the Second World War, that Indigenous veterans were allowed to lay Remembrance Day wreaths at the National War Memorial to remember and honour their dead comrades.

At the time of the First World War, status Indians were exempt from conscription because they were not considered "citizens" of Canada and did not have the right to vote. To serve in the Canadian Air Force or Canadian Navy, you had to be "of pure European descent"; this restriction was rescinded in 1940 for the Air Force and 1943 for the Navy.

Being exempt from conscription did not dissuade status Indians from wanting to fight in the First World War. It is estimated that 4,000, or one in three able bodied status Indian men, volunteered to fight; of that number, approximately 300 died. By 1942, compulsory overseas service was implemented, and, in 1943, the government declared that as British subjects, "all able Native men of military age" (Inuit People remained exempt from conscription) could be called up for training and service. Many bands protested with marches and petitions to Ottawa. The issue was raised several times in the House of Commons, and, in 1944, the decision was made by the war cabinet committee to exempt status Indians who had been assured during treaty negotiations that they would not be involved in British battles.

During the Second World War, more than 3,000 enlisted (of which over 200 died) and those that remained in Canada supported the war effort monetarily.

Between the two world wars, some Indian reserve land was sold to the Soldier Settlement Board for veterans who wished to farm, by Order-in-Council (PC, 393 of 16, February, 1918). Many more thousands of acres were leased to non-Indigenous farmers for up to five years to promote greater agricultural production for the war effort.

After the First World War, Status Indian veterans did not receive the same assistance as other returned soldiers under the War Veterans Allowance Act—this policy endured from 1932 until 1936. Many Status Indian veterans from the Second World War found that, when they returned home after fighting overseas for Canada, they were no longer considered Status Indians because the *Indian Act* specified that Indians absent from the reserve for four years were no longer Status Indians.

Many Indigenous soldiers had to become enfranchised before they could sign up to fight in the Second World War, which meant that when they returned to their home communities, they no longer had Indian status.

Status Indian war veterans did not have the right to obtain other benefits available to non-Indigenous veterans due to *Indian Act* restrictions. Between 1932 and 1936, Status Indian veterans on reserves in need of help were to be treated like other Status Indians on reserves, rather than as veterans. Many Second World War veterans, including Tommy George Prince (the most decorated Indigenous war veteran, whose medals included the American Silver Star and six service medals), re-enlisted for the Korean War simply because they were unable to re-enter their previous lives. The lives of numerous Indigenous veterans ended in despair and poverty.

Indian Hospitals[13]

The history of Indian hospitals (1920s–1980s) in Canada is not as well-known as that of residential schools, but is as horrific in both its actions and the implication of those actions. This aspect of Canadian history shows that care for the health of Indians was never a priority and never on par with the care available for Europeans. Health care for Indians, such as it was, was motivated by a number of factors that range from keeping as many patients "interned" as possible to maintain government funding, to ensure a steady number of subjects for medical and nutritional experiments, and to ensure that the European population was protected from exposure to "Indian tuberculosis."

Segregated medical treatment for Indian patients was the norm in community hospitals where they were treated in the basement or "Indian annexes," but the outbreak of tuberculosis (TB) introduced segregation on a larger scale.

"Death rates in the 1930s and 1940s were in excess of 700 deaths per 100,000 persons, among the highest ever reported in a human population ... Tragically, TB death rates among children in residential schools were even worse."[14]

It is important to understand the symbiotic connection between the high incidence of TB in Indians and residential schools. Many of the residential schools, with their overcrowding, malnutrition, and lack of heat, were fertile sites for the rampant spread of the highly communicable tuberculosis virus. Children who became infected were sent to the Indian hospitals, and when they showed signs of recovery, were sent back to the residential school. This mutually beneficial arrangement maintained the numbers and funding of both organizations.

Just as it was legal under the *Indian Act*, to apprehend Indian children and put them in segregated (residential) schools, it was legal to apprehend Indians suspected of having TB and segregate or quarantine them. Interestingly, that part of the Act remains today. In some centres, the local doctor was also the Indian agent.

INDIAN ACT, 1876
REGULATIONS
Marginal note: Regulations
- 73. (1) The Governor in Council may make regulations
- *(h)* provide compulsory hospitalization and treatment for infectious diseases among Indians;

INDIAN ACT, 1985
Regulations
- 73 (1) The Governor in Council may make regulations
- (h) to provide compulsory hospitalization and treatment for infectious diseases among Indians;

There also were examples of experimental treatment of tuberculosis. Records were poorly kept, but some patients speak of having a lung removed which involved having sections of their ribs connecting to their spines cut off—an operation routinely performed with just a local anesthetic. As ribs don't regenerate, those who suffered through and survived these operations were left crippled, both physically and emotionally.

The bacillus-Calmette-Guerin (BCG) vaccine for tuberculosis was tested on patients in the Fort Qu'Appelle Sanatorium in the early 1930s by Dr. R. George Ferguson:

"In 1933 Ferguson, funded by Indian Affairs and the National Research Council, began an experimental vaccine trial on local Aboriginal infants. His twelve-year study was an apparent success: only six of the 306 children in the vaccinated group developed tuberculosis and two died; while 29 of the 303 in the control group developed tuberculosis and nine died. But Ferguson's research also revealed that 77 of the 609 children in the trial, or more than 12 percent, died before their first birthday, while only four of these were tuberculosis deaths (two in each of the vaccinated and control groups.) In all, nearly one-fifth of the children in the trial died from other diseases, mostly gastroenteritis and pneumonia. Poverty posed the greatest threat to children, but unlike tuberculosis, it did not spread to white communities. BCG lived up to its promise to control tuberculosis while leaving untouched the socio-economic conditions that led to its rise."[15]

One of the founding principles supporting the establishment of hospitals for the sole treatment of Indians was that they would be run cost efficiently. That underlying principle led to the majority of staff being poorly trained health care workers. Doctors were not interested in working in remote, isolated, poorly funded, inadequate Indian hospitals when they could work in major centres.

The buildings were often redundant military barracks haphazardly repurposed as hospitals. These buildings generally lacked the most basic features of hospital facilities of the era and were run with inadequate laundries, poorly equipped kitchens, and subpar maintenance—inadequacies that exacerbated the symptoms of the patients.

As with residential schools, Indian hospitals are not ancient history, The lingering impact of undergoing "treatment" at an Indian hospital has resulted in many elderly Indians having a deeply rooted fear and mistrust of medical personnel. It could also be argued that roots of racism in the medical system today towards Indian patients has its roots in the history of Indian hospitals.

Inuit (formerly Eskimo)

It should also be noted in this time that Inuit, formerly called Eskimos (Eskimo is considered derogatory in Canada, but is still in use in Alaska), were being forcibly settled as part of the assimilation process. This was achieved via the Inuit dog sled program. Another action was to assign identification tags:

"In Inuit tradition, a child is not considered to be a complete person until they receive an *atiq* or 'soulname,' usually given at birth. The construction of a subject's identity therefore is a complex process involving the historical customs of 'naming,' kinship practices, as well as spiritual beliefs. The subject's identity is thus composed of multiple layers, as the following narrative suggests:

No child is only a child. If I give my grandfather's *atiq* to my baby daughter, she is my grandfather. I will call her *ataatassiaq*, grandfather. She is entitled to call me grandson."[16]

Inuit, until the 20th century, were pretty much overlooked by the rest of the world and had few interactions with Europeans apart from infrequent encounters with explorers and whalers. That all changed when fur traders began to move further north, and with them came trading posts, the RCMP, missionaries, government agencies . . . and bureaucracy. With the bureaucracy came the inevitable desire for lists of who was who in the vast tundra.

The new northerners had trouble pronouncing and spelling Inuk names and couldn't fathom the traditional naming system that was, to them, illogical. The first wave of efforts to establish a naming system was driven by the missionaries. Their plan was for the population to be baptized and given Christian names. This was quite well received, but Inuit in turn had trouble pronouncing and translating the new names into syllabic writing script so they modified their new names. They also continued to use their traditional names, which caused quite a bit of confusion for government officials, medical personnel, and RCMP.

By 1929, after many years of frustration and confusion, government officials considered and introduced various ways to devise a universal system of identification. Some attempts were so very poorly planned and executed they simply exacerbated the confusion around identities. As was typical of the time, little regard was paid to the impact on Inuit of having their soulname erased.

"The importance of the Eskimo name is something I have spoken of before. It is very important for each individual to be properly identified. In the Eskimo tradition it had an even greater significance, and there is a persistence of the attitude derived from those traditional beliefs, whereby the name is the soul and the soul is the name. So if you misuse someone's name, you not only damage his own personal identity in the existing society but you also damage his immortal soul." [17]

Here's a timeline of suggested naming systems:

1929—standardization spelling of names

1932—separate files for each Inuk showing name in English and syllabic characters, along with fingerprints

1933—fingerprinting by the RCMP of Inuit who received medical assistance

1935—binominal system of names. The head of each family to select a common name for his family

1935—identification disc, similar to that used in the army, stamped with a letter and a number

The identification disc system was adopted in 1941. The plan was for each Inuk to be assigned a number on a disc which was to be worn at all times or sewn into clothing. The numbers were used in all official documentation, including the salutation in letters. This identification system was fraught with issues including Inuit destroying the discs, shortages of the discs which meant many people were not registered, and inconsistent numbering. Also, the registration records of babies born before the advent of the disc were not updated with the new numbers and many babies born after 1941 were also not registered due to the shortage of discs in certain regions. Inconsistent reporting and registering deaths contributed to the confusion.

Identification became more critical in 1945 with the introduction of the Children's Allowance program (later known as Family Allowance, but currently known as Child Benefit program)—Canada's first universal welfare program. Accurate family records were required for the issuance of the monthly payment. The existing registration system was a mess so "all discs were recalled and new ones were issued. The Canadian Arctic and Northern Quebec were divided into twelve districts, with three districts in the west (W1, W2 and W3) and nine districts in the east (E1 to E9). The new disks incorporated an alphanumeric identifier, reflecting the geographic region Inuit inhabited, as well as their unique four-digit number."[18]

In 1968, the Northwest Territories Government (NWT) introduced "Project Surname," an initiative intended to persuade all Inuk adults to adopt and register a family name, which, along with their given names, was given a standardized spelling. By 1972, all Inuit within the NWT were registered and the disc system was discontinued. The disc system was gradually phased out in other regions.

The Right to Vote

The right to vote, which most Canadians take for granted, was a hard-fought battle for Indigenous Peoples. In most parts of Canada, Status Indians were offered the right to vote at the time of Confederation—but only if they gave up their treaty rights and Indian status. Understandably, few were willing to do this. Métis People were not excluded from voting, as few were covered by treaties; therefore, there was nothing to justify disqualifying them. Inuit also were excluded and no steps were taken to include them since most communities were geographically isolated. So, in the absence of special efforts to enable them to vote, they had no means of exercising the franchise.

Long before contact with Europeans, Indigenous Peoples had elaborate systems of government, therefore many viewed the nineteenth century proposal for enfranchisement (the granting of the right to vote to citizens) unfavourably for two reasons: first, it would mean the termination of their recognition as distinct Nations or People (as signified by treaties with France, Great Britain, and, later, Canada), which would mean the beginning of their assimilation into non-Indigenous society; and, secondly, it would mean voting in a system of government that was alien to the traditions, conventions, and practices of governance of many Status Indians. Voting was also considered redundant as a traditional, effective system was already in place for choosing leaders and governing Nations.

Proposals to offer the franchise date back to at least 1885, but were met with hostility within the federal government. The status quo endured for nearly a century as there was little pressure to extend the franchise—although it was extended in 1924 to Indigenous veterans of the First World War, including on-reserve veterans.

The fact that so many Indigenous People served with distinction in the Second World War was one of the reasons why it was concluded that the time had come for all Indigenous People to have the full rights of citizenship. In 1948, a parliamentary committee recommended that the right to vote be extended to all Indigenous Peoples. The federal government did extend the franchise to Inuit, who did not have treaties or reserves so were legally considered "ordinary citizens," but Status Indians who wanted to vote would still have to waive their right to tax exemptions; given the significance of this treaty right, few did so.

It was not until 1960, under the leadership of Prime Minister John Diefenbaker, that Status Indians were offered the franchise without having to give up any treaty rights in exchange.

The Sixties Scoop

The term "Sixties Scoop" refers to the period from 1961 through to the 1980s that saw an astounding number of Indigenous babies and children literally scooped from the arms of their parents and placed in boarding schools or the homes of middle-class Euro-Canadian families. This period of child apprehension arose in the wake of the closing of the residential schools.

The phasing out of residential schools began in the 1950s due to a growing public awareness of the devastating impacts on the children, families, and communities. The assimilation program did not die out at that time, however; it simply deployed a different tactic.

In 1951, the *Indian Act* was amended to allow provincial governments to provide services to Indigenous people in areas where the federal government formerly had not, and these new services included child protection. In British Columbia in 1952, less than 30 Indigenous children were in provincial care; by 1964, nearly 1,500 (or 34 percent of all children in provincial care) were Indigenous. Residential schools continued under the guise of boarding schools for the children of families who were deemed incapable of caring for their children. Not all the children were placed in boarding schools—many were adopted by non-Indigenous families and raised within that culture.

"Sixties scoop" was coined by Patrick Johnston who wrote the "Native Children and the Child Welfare System" report in 1983. In his report, Johnston quotes a social worker who said "with tears in her eyes—that it was a common practise in B.C. in the mid-sixties to "scoop" from their mothers on reserves almost all newly born children. She was crying because she realized—20 years later—what a mistake that had been."

Social workers were not expected or required to have experience, skills, or knowledge relevant to the traditions, culture, or history of the Indigenous communities within their jurisdiction. Their evaluation of a nurturing and safe family life was based upon their own, often middle-class Euro-Canadian perspective—traditional Indigenous family life and diet were generally neither understood, valued, nor recognized. That perspective, when viewing the poverty, unemployment, and substance abuse that affected many Indigenous communities led to the assumption that the children were not receiving adequate care and so were removed—frequently without warning or the consent of the parents. This scooping of children without consent continued in B.C. until 1980 at which time the Child, Family and Community Services Act stipulated that social workers were required to notify band council if a child were to be removed.

The apprehension of children from their families and communities and placement in boarding schools or adopted out to non-Indigenous families is considered "cultural genocide" under the UN Convention of Genocide (1948). Article 2(e) states:

> "forcibly transferring children of the group to another group" constituted cultural genocide when the intent is to destroy a culture. Protection of children of Indigenous Peoples was further enhanced by the **United Nations Declaration on the**

Rights of Indigenous Peoples, Article 7 that states "Indigenous peoples have the collective right to live in freedom, peace and security as distinct peoples and shall not be subjected to any act of genocide or any other act of violence, including forcibly removing children of the group to another group."

If you do the math, you will realize just how many generations of people in Canada have been affected by the assimilation programs of the *Indian Act*.

The White Paper, 1969

In 1969, the government of Canada introduced the Statement of the Government of Canada on Indian policy (The White Paper, 1969) which called for the removal of the *Indian Act,* the transfer of reserve lands to individuals, and the removal of the federal government's fiduciary duty. The White Paper, 1969 was regarded as the final instrument in the long-standing policy of Indian assimilation. Indigenous leaders vehemently opposed the imposition of The White Paper, 1969 recommendations as they believed the recommendations would result in significantly worse living conditions than those that existed in the era that followed the residential school debacle.

Confronted by Indigenous opposition to the White Paper from coast to coast, the federal government withdrew the initiative in 1971, replacing it with the "Core Funding Program"—supplying Indigenous groups with resources to promote their causes through research, publication, and legal action.

Shortly thereafter came a commitment by the then-Minister of Indian Affairs, Jean Chrétien, to begin negotiations with the Nisga'a Nation and to begin the process of treaty-making in northern Canada. In 2000, as the Prime Minister of Canada, Jean Chrétien saw the completion of the *Nisga'a Final Agreement*, bringing the negotiations that he initiated to fruition.

At the Liberal Party of Canada biennial convention in February 2014, party members voted to reject the White Paper, 1969.

C. 1982—WARDS TO NATIONS

The Constitution Act, 1982

In 1982, the Government of Canada patriated the Canadian Constitution, and, in so doing, formally entrenched Aboriginal and treaty rights in the supreme law of Canada.

Section 35 of the *Constitution Act, 1982* provides:

"35(1) The existing aboriginal and treaty rights of the aboriginal people in Canada are hereby recognized and affirmed.

(2) In this Act, "Aboriginal Peoples of Canada "includes the Indian, Inuit, and Métis Peoples of Canada.

(3) For greater certainty, in subsection (1), "treaty rights" includes rights that now exist by way of land claims agreements or may be so acquired.

(4) Notwithstanding any other provision of this act, the aboriginal and treaty rights referred to in subsection (1) are guaranteed equally to male and female persons."[1]

Section 35 neither confirms nor creates absolute Aboriginal rights. It does confirm "existing Aboriginal or treaty rights" that had not been extinguished by surrender or legislation before 1982.

On the other hand, Aboriginal and treaty rights existing after proclamation of the *Constitution Act, 1982* now receive significant legal protection under section 35. Existing Aboriginal land rights can no longer be extinguished without the consent of those Aboriginal Peoples holding interests in those lands. Aboriginal consent may be required to give effect to legislation purporting to extinguish Aboriginal land rights, even if compensation is paid. Finally, government regulation of Aboriginal land rights may still be possible, if appropriate and meaningful consultation is undertaken with the affected Aboriginal communities.

The patriation of the Constitution has contributed to the creation of space for Canada's Aboriginal Peoples and the governments to work towards the recognition, respect, and reconciliation of Aboriginal rights and title.

The patriated Constitution also set the stage for the Supreme Court of Canada to begin to weigh in on issues related to Aboriginal rights and title. The underlying belief was that once treaty and Aboriginal rights were recognized in the Constitution as "constitutional rights" that recognition provided a legal status protecting Aboriginal rights and title. In reality, the burden fell upon Aboriginal Peoples to define, primarily through litigation, the nature and quality of those rights.

Lack of Political Will: The Courts Lead the Way

It is fair to say that, until recently, there has been a conspicuous lack of political will in Canada for dealing with Aboriginal issues such as land claims and self-government. Many in the body politic have believed that Aboriginal Peoples should be treated as equal to other Canadians and that they shouldn't have "special rights." This "equality" ideology has made it tough for legislators to come up with legislative solutions that would be acceptable to Aboriginal Peoples, without reducing the government's prospects for re-election. So, given their lack of political strength, what could Aboriginal Peoples do to advance their land claims and pursuit of self-government? They could, and did, turn to the courts for support—and we have seen the Supreme Court of Canada leading the way toward reform ever since.

Beginning with the ground-breaking *Calder* case in 1973, the Supreme Court of Canada has used a series of important decisions to define and explain Aboriginal rights and title in Canada. The thread of reasoning that runs through this line of cases has woven the concept of unextinguished Aboriginal title deep into the fabric of Canadian law, which has induced both the federal and provincial governments to undertake meaningful treaty-making, and has greatly strengthened Aboriginal Peoples negotiating positions.

Calder,[2] **Supreme Court of Canada, 1973**

In the *Calder* case, the Nisga'a Tribal Council asked the courts to support their claim that Aboriginal title had never been extinguished in the Nass Valley, near Prince Rupert. Although the Supreme Court of Canada ultimately ruled against the Nisga'a on a technicality, the case is historic because, for the first time, Canada's highest court ruled that Aboriginal title was rooted in the "long-time occupation, possession, and use" of traditional territories. As such, Aboriginal title existed at the time of original contact with Europeans, and at the time of formal assertion of British sovereignty in 1846.[3]

Shortly after the *Calder* decision, the Canadian government agreed to begin negotiating with the Nisga'a on their "Land Question," and with northern Aboriginal Peoples on treaties to define their rights to land and resources.

Guerin,[4] **Supreme Court of Canada, 1984**

In 1955, the Musqueam First Nation approved a surrender "in trust" of some of its reserve land in the city of Vancouver, for the purpose of a lease to the Shaughnessy Golf and Country Club. The lease transaction had been discussed in detail with the band and band consent had been given based on those discussions. The Crown subsequently concluded a lease on terms substantially different and less advantageous to the Musqueam. The true terms of the lease were not disclosed to the band until 1970.

In *Guerin*, the judgment of Chief Justice Brian Dickson extended *Calder* to describe Aboriginal interest in land as a "pre-existing legal right not created by the *Royal Proclamation* ... the *Indian Act* ... or any other executive order or legislative provision."

The Supreme Court ruled that the federal government had a "fiduciary responsibility" for Aboriginal people—that is, a responsibility to safeguard Aboriginal interests. This duty placed the government under a legal obligation to manage Aboriginal lands as a prudent person would when dealing with his/her own property. The Court held the government had breached this fiduciary duty and awarded damages of $10 million to the Musqueam First Nation.

Martin,[5] Supreme Court & Court of Appeal of British Columbia, 1985—ongoing (the Meares Island Case)

In 1984, members of the Nuu-chah-nulth First Nation and other protesters blocked MacMillan Bloedel's access to its timber berth on Meares Island. The Province of British Columbia regarded the vast majority of the island as Crown land, but the protesters claimed that allowing logging on Meares Island interfered with Aboriginal title. A court injunction was sought to halt MacMillan Bloedel's operations until the claim was resolved.

The B.C. Supreme Court denied the request, but the B.C. Court of Appeal (which does not usually grant leave to hear appeals in such injunction cases)[6] agreed to hear the application. In granting the injunction in a three to two decision, the majority gave some pointed feedback to the provincial Crown. Justice Seaton said:

> "It has ... been suggested that a decision favourable to the Indians will cast a huge doubt on the tenure that is the basis for the huge investment that has been made and is being made ... There is a problem about tenure that has not been attended to in the past. We are being asked to ignore the problem as [the province of British Columbia has] ignored it. I am not willing to do that."[7] (emphasis added)

Justice MacFarlane was even blunter in calling for meaningful treaty-making negotiations:

> "The fact that there is an issue between the Indians and the province based on Aboriginal claims should not come as a surprise to anyone. Those claims have been advanced by the Indians for many years. They were advanced in [the Calder case] and half the court thought they had some substance ... **I think it is fair to say that, in the end, the public anticipates that the claims will be resolved by negotiations and by settlement. This judicial proceeding is but a small part of the whole process which will ultimately find its solutions in a reasonable exchange between governments and the Indian nations.**"[8] (emphasis added)

The *Martin (Meares Island)* case was adjourned by agreement of the Nuu-chah-nulth First Nation, MacMillan Bloedel, and the governments of British Columbia and Canada. The injunction on logging is still in effect and none of the parties have requested resumption of the trial. As a result of *Martin*, B.C.'s provincial Ministry of Native Affairs was created in 1988.[9] By 1989, public support for the government's entry into treaty negotiations had reached 80%, and Social Credit Premier Vander Zalm appointed a Native Affairs Advisory Committee to consider the government's options. By the fall of 1990, following the Mohawk blockades at Oka and Kahnawake, and further Aboriginal blockades across the country (particularly in Alberta and B.C.), Premier Vander Zalm announced that his government would commence negotiations with B.C.'s Aboriginal and First Nations (still without acknowledging Aboriginal title).

Sparrow,[10] Supreme Court of Canada, 1990

In the *Sparrow* case, a member of the Musqueam First Nation appealed his conviction on a charge of fishing with a longer drift net than permitted by the terms of the band's fishing license under the *Fisheries Act*. He based his appeal on the argument that the restriction on net length was invalid because it was inconsistent with section 35 of the *Constitution Act, 1982*[11]—the section of the *Act* that recognizes and affirms existing Aboriginal and treaty rights.

The *Sparrow* case was the first opportunity for the Supreme Court of Canada to interpret what section 35 actually meant. In overturning Sparrow's conviction, the Court ruled that the *Constitution Act* provides "a strong measure of protection" for Aboriginal rights, and that any proposed government regulations that infringe on the exercise of those rights must be constitutionally justified. The two-part *Sparrow* test for determining whether an infringement can be justified is:

1. the government must be acting pursuant to a valid legislative object; and
2. the government's actions must be consistent with its fiduciary duty toward Aboriginal Peoples.

If a valid legislative object is established, assessment of whether the government's actions are consistent with that fiduciary duty between the Crown and Aboriginal Peoples requires that three questions be addressed:

1. Has there been as "little infringement as possible" in order to achieve the intended result?

2. In a case of expropriation, has fair compensation been paid?
3. Has the particular Aboriginal People been consulted?

The *Sparrow* justification test applies beyond Aboriginal rights to include treaty rights and Aboriginal title as well.

The *Sparrow* Court further ruled that:

- Aboriginal and treaty rights are capable of evolving over time and must be interpreted in a generous and liberal manner.
- Governments may regulate existing Aboriginal rights only for a compelling and substantial objective, such as the conservation and management of resources.
- After conservation goals are met, Aboriginal Peoples must be given priority to fish for food over other user groups.

Delgamuukw,[12] Court of Appeal of British Columbia; Supreme Court of Canada, 1984-1997

The *Delgamuukw* cases are critical pieces of the Constitutional puzzle of Aboriginal rights and title for British Columbia and all of Canada. Together, the three *Delgamuukw* decisions, summarized below, raise a number of important issues strongly addressed in the Supreme Court of Canada's 2004 *Haida Nation*[13] decision, and provide a good foundation for our review of that case.

In 1984, 35 Gitxsan and 13 Wet'suwet'en Hereditary Chiefs asked the Supreme Court of British Columbia to recognize their ownership of 57,000 square kilometres of land in north-western B.C., to confirm their right to govern their traditional territories, and to award compensation for loss of their lands and resources. The Gitxsan and Wet'suwet'en elected to proceed with trial by judge alone (rather than by judge and jury) and submitted an enormous body of oral and written evidence[14] regarding the nature and duration of their use and occupation of their traditional lands.

In his reasons for judgment released in 1991, Chief Justice McEachern left open the possibility that Aboriginal rights may arise through the use and occupation of specific lands for Aboriginal purposes for an indefinite (and lengthy) period prior to British sovereignty. However, he ruled that the Crown had extinguished any such Aboriginal rights by its imposition of complete dominion over the Colonial territory prior to joining Confederation in 1871. The Gitxsan and Wet'suwet'en appealed.

In 1993, the B.C. Court of Appeal reversed much of the lower court's decision and ruled instead that the Gitxsan and Wet'suwet'en peoples do have "unextinguished non-exclusive Aboriginal rights, other than a right of ownership," to much of their traditional territory. In addition, the appeal court Justices strongly recommended that the scope and content of those rights would best be defined through negotiation rather than litigation. The British Columbia government appealed to the Supreme Court of Canada.

On December 11, 1997, a unanimous Supreme Court of Canada handed down its much-studied *Delgamuukw* judgment, providing some important definition and description of Aboriginal title, affirming the legal validity of Aboriginal oral history, and clarifying the nature of the Crown's duties of consultation and accommodation in the context of infringement of Aboriginal rights.

This landmark ruling confirmed the existence of Aboriginal rights and title and provided a test to prove them. The Court didn't declare Delgamuukw the winner, but sent the parties back to a lower court because of errors in how the case was brought forward. *Delgamuukw* established Aboriginal title as an encumbrance on the Crown's ultimate title that contains an inescapable economic component: driving a Crown duty of consultation that can include financial compensation for infringement of rights and title, and that can mean the full consent of an Aboriginal Nation whose core usage rights (such as hunting and fishing) are at stake.

Aboriginal Title

Chief Justice Lamer's judgment for the Court provided the most comprehensive Supreme Court description of Aboriginal title seen to date:

> "[A]boriginal title encompasses the right to exclusive use and occupation of the land held pursuant to that title. (at para. 117) What aboriginal title confers in the right to the land itself. (at para. 138) [A]boriginal title encompasses the right to exclusive use and occupation of land; second, aboriginal title encompasses the right to choose to what uses land can be put, subject to the ultimate limit that those uses cannot destroy the ability of the land to sustain future generations of aboriginal people; and third, that lands held pursuant to aboriginal title have an inescapable economic component." (at para. 166, emphasis in original)

That "inescapable economic component" has two elements: on the one hand, it means that the need to develop natural resources can, in principle, justify infringement of Aboriginal title by the Province (raising the duty to consult and accommodate); on the other hand, it means that an Aboriginal group can choose economic uses for its land that are not confined to its culture or historical practices.

The Court set out three components as the basis for a successful claim of Aboriginal title:

- The land must have been occupied prior to European sovereignty (in British Columbia, that was 1849);
- If the proof of pre-sovereignty occupation to be relied upon is "current possession," then there must be continuity between pre-sovereignty and present occupation; and
- At the time that European sovereignty was established, Aboriginal occupation must have been exclusive, or with provision for shared exclusivity.

The Court also ruled that Aboriginal title remains an encumbrance on Provincial Crown where it has not been surrendered to or otherwise extinguished by the federal government—meaning that **Aboriginal title cannot be surrendered to the Province**.

Oral History

Chief Justice Lamer found that the trial judge erred in refusing to take into account the Aboriginal oral histories presented to the court by the Gitxsan and Wet'suwet'en to establish use and occupation of their traditional territories, and concluded:

> "The trial judge, after refusing to admit, or giving no independent weight to these oral histories, reached the conclusion that the appellants had not demonstrated the requisite degree of occupation for 'ownership.' Had the trial judge assessed the oral histories correctly, his conclusions on these issues of fact might have been very different." (at para. 107)[15]

Infringement of Aboriginal Rights and Crown Duty of Consultation

The Court confirmed its ruling in *Sparrow*[16] that Aboriginal title is not absolute and may be infringed upon by both federal and provincial governments, provided that the two-part *Sparrow* justification test is met.

In elaborating on the implication and weight of that special fiduciary duty of the Crown to look after the best interests of Aboriginal Peoples, the Supreme Court also addressed the issue of **consultation**:

> "The fiduciary duty between the Crown and Aboriginal Peoples may be satisfied by the involvement of Aboriginal Peoples in decisions taken with respect to their lands. There is always a duty of consultation. Whether the Aboriginal group has been consulted is relevant in determining whether the infringement of Aboriginal

title is justified ... The nature and scope of the duty of consultation will vary with the circumstances. In occasional cases, when the breach is less serious or relatively minor, it will be no more than a duty to discuss important decisions that will be taken with respect to lands held pursuant to Aboriginal title ... The minimum acceptable standard is consultation [that] must be in good faith, and with the intention of substantially addressing the concerns of the Aboriginal Peoples whose lands are at issue. In most cases, it will be significantly deeper than mere consultation. Some cases may even require the full consent of an Aboriginal nation, particularly when provinces enact hunting and fishing regulations in relation to aboriginal lands."[17] (emphasis added)

The Court went further to note that the "inescapable economic component" of Aboriginal title referred to earlier means that compensation will be required when that title is infringed. The amount and nature of the compensation required will depend on the context—i.e. on " ... the nature of the Aboriginal title affected, the severity of the infringement, and the extent to which Aboriginal interests have been accommodated."[18]

Haida Nation v. British Columbia (Minister of Forests)[19] —Supreme Court of Canada, 2004

The Council of the Haida Nation brought an action against the Provincial Crown and Weyerhaeuser Company Limited for not properly consulting with the Haida Nation when renewing a tree farm licence on Haida Gwaii. Tree Farm Licence 39, issued to Weyerhaeuser, contained several areas of old growth red cedar—a culturally significant tree used for totem poles, canoes, and log houses. The Haida Nation wanted large areas of old growth forest protected from clear cutting and its potential detrimental effects on land, watershed, fish, and wildlife.

By a unanimous (7-0) decision delivered by Chief Justice McLachlin, the Supreme Court of Canada went a long way toward providing further clarity and direction arising from *Delgamuukw* decision and the Court of Appeal decisions in *Haida Nation* and *Taku River Tlingit*. The strongly worded judgment makes two issues very clear. First, both orders of government have an inescapable Constitutional duty to consult and accommodate Aboriginal communities in a manner that is meaningful, timely, and reflective of the "honour of the Crown," regarding potential infringement on an Aboriginal right or title. Second, that duty rests with the Crown; it cannot be delegated to and does not otherwise extend to third parties (i.e. to industry).

The Crown's Duty to Consult and Accommodate

The Court's thorough and clear explanation of the source, nature, and object of the duties of consultation and accommodation sent a strong message to government, and provided valuable guidance to both industry and Aboriginal leadership for successful engagement.

> **Source of the Duty**—"The government's duty to consult with Aboriginal Peoples and accommodate their interests is grounded in the honour of the Crown. The honour of the Crown is always at stake in its dealing with Aboriginal Peoples... The historical roots of the principle of the honour of the Crown suggest that it must be understood generously in order to reflect the underlying realities from which it stems. In all its dealings with Aboriginal Peoples, from the assertion of sovereignty to the resolution of claims and the implementation of treaties, the Crown must act honourably. Nothing less is required if we are to achieve 'the reconciliation of the pre-existence of Aboriginal societies with the sovereignty of the Crown.'"(Delgamuukw at para. 186)[20]

These opening statements from the Court's analysis of the "source of a duty to consult and accommodate" cut to the heart of the matter. Ultimately, that "reconciliation of the pre-existence of Aboriginal societies with the sovereignty of the Crown" has to be found before the legacy of expropriation and assimilation can be put behind us, and before lasting business certainty can be achieved in Canada.

When the Duty to Consult Arises

The Province presented its traditional argument that any duty of consultation or accommodation that it might have does not arise unless and until a claim of Aboriginal rights or title is proven. The Court flatly rejected that view:

> "The foundation of the duty in the Crown's honour and the goal of reconciliation, suggest that the duty arises when the Crown has knowledge, real or constructive, of the potential existence of the Aboriginal right or title and contemplates conduct that might adversely affect it."[21]

Scope and Content of the Duty to Consult and Accommodate

If the duty arises before a claim of Aboriginal rights or title is proven, how is the Crown (and industry, as a matter of good business relations) to know what range and depth of consultation (and perhaps accommodation) is appropriate?

"... [I]t will frequently be possible to reach an idea of the asserted rights and of their strength sufficient to trigger an obligation to consult and accommodate, short of final judicial determination or settlement. To facilitate this determination, claimants should outline their claims with clarity, focusing on the scope and nature of the Aboriginal rights they assert and on the alleged infringements...

"There is a distinction between knowledge sufficient to trigger a duty to consult and, if appropriate, accommodate, and the content or scope of the duty in a particular case. The content of the duty, however, varies with the circumstances... A dubious or peripheral claim may attract a mere duty of notice, while a stronger claim may attract more stringent duties... **Parties can assess these matters, and if they cannot agree, tribunals and courts can assist. Difficulties associated with the absence of proof and definitions of claims are addressed by assigning appropriate content to the duty, not by denying the existence of the duty.**"[22] (emphasis added)

This means that the Crown's duty to consult and accommodate regarding potential infringement on claims of Aboriginal rights and title is **proportionate** to the strength of the particular claim and to the potential harm that may be caused to that claim by the proposed policy or action.

Accommodation: Meaning and Mutual Responsibility

The Supreme Court also provided valuable clarification of the working meaning of "accommodation," and set out some pointed advice clearly intended for both government and Aboriginal leaders:

"At all stages, good faith on both sides is required. The common thread on the Crown's part must be 'the intention of substantially addressing [Aboriginal] concerns' as they are raised (*Delgamuukw* at para. 168), through a meaningful process of consultation. As for Aboriginal claimants, they must not frustrate the Crown's reasonable good faith attempts, nor should they take unreasonable positions to thwart government from making decisions or acting in cases where, despite meaningful consultation, agreement is not reached ... The process does not give Aboriginal groups a veto over what can be done with land pending final proof of the claim. The Aboriginal 'consent' spoken of in *Delgamuukw* is appropriate only in cases of established rights, and then by no means in every case. Rather, what is required is a process of balancing interests, of give and take."[23]

Who Owes the Duty?

The Supreme Court determined that the Crown must bear sole responsibility for consultation and accommodation regarding the possibility of infringement of Aboriginal rights or title by its actions, or by actions performed under its licence:

> "[T]he duty to consult and accommodate... flows from the Crown's assumption of sovereignty over lands and resources formerly held by the Aboriginal group... The Crown alone remains legally responsible for the consequences of its actions and interactions with third parties, that affect Aboriginal interests. The Crown may delegate procedural aspects of consultation to industry proponents seeking a particular development; this not infrequently done in environmental assessments. Similarly, the terms of T.F.L. 39 mandated Weyerhaeuser to specify measures that it would take to identify and consult with 'aboriginal people claiming an aboriginal interest in or to the area '(Tree Farm Licence No. 39, Haida Tree Farm Licence, para. 2.09(g)(ii)). **However, the ultimate legal responsibility for consultation and accommodation rests with the Crown. The honour of the Crown cannot be delegated.**"[24] (emphasis added)

It is important to note that this decision leaves industry and other third parties fully accountable for their own actions in dealing with Aboriginal rights and title:

> "The fact that third parties are under no duty to consult or accommodate Aboriginal concerns does not mean that they can never be accountable to Aboriginal Peoples. If they act negligently in circumstances where they owe Aboriginal Peoples a duty of care, or if they breach contracts with Aboriginal Peoples or deal with them dishonestly, they may be held legally liable."[25]

While the Court didn't spell out the "circumstances where third parties may owe Aboriginal Peoples a duty of care," the clarity of this Supreme Court definition of the depth and scope of the Crown's duty to consult and to accommodate will certainly inform third parties of a duty of care."Foreseeability" of the harm that may be caused by one's actions to someone owed a duty of care goes to the heart of liability in the law of negligence."Consultation and accommodation" remains prudent business practice in situations where Aboriginal rights or title (whether claimed or confirmed) may be infringed upon by business decisions or actions.

The Province's Duty to Consult, Accommodate, and Negotiate

B.C.'s argument that any duty to consult or accommodate belongs solely to the federal government was dismissed:

> "... [T]he Province took [its] interest in the land subject to 'any interest other than that of the Province in the same.' The duty to consult and accommodate here at issue is grounded in the assertion of Crown sovereignty which pre-dated the Union. It follows that the Province took the lands subject to this duty. It cannot therefore claim that s. 35 [of the *Constitution Act, 1982*] deprives it of powers it would otherwise have enjoyed."[26]

Taku River Tlingit First Nation v. British Columbia (Project Assessment Director)[27]— Supreme Court of Canada, 2004

Applying *Haida Nation*, the Court ruled that the Crown owed a duty to consult meaningfully with the Taku River Tlingit First Nation (TRTFN) regarding the decision to reopen the Tulsequah Chief Mine, and to permit Redfern Resources Ltd. (the mine operator) to build a 160 kilometre access road through a portion of their traditional territory. However, the Supreme Court also found that the duty of consultation was met by TRTFN's extensive involvement in the three and a half year review process conducted under B.C.'s Environmental Assessment Act.

THERE HAVE BEEN many more cases in the provincial courts across Canada and in the Supreme Court of Canada considering Aboriginal rights and title. This review is of the key Supreme Court rulings on Aboriginal rights and title, going back to *Calder*. These cases were chosen to illustrate the legal foundation built by the Court outlining the Crown's duty of consultation, accommodation, and negotiation. There is still much discussion and direction to be provided by the court on Aboriginal rights and title. The underlying key message of the Supreme Court in all of these cases has been that these issues are best negotiated rather than litigated.

All of the previous cases have their roots in British Columbia. It may appear that we have a bias towards legal decisions from the West Coast, but that is not the case. Unlike the rest of Canada, where treaties had been entered into between First Nations and Canada, B.C. was relatively untouched. There are a few exceptions in the far northeast section of the province and southern Vancouver Island's Douglas Treaties. It is this significant difference that led First Nations in B.C., and both the federal and provincial governments, to seek clarification from the Supreme Court of Canada as to the parties' respective rights, title, and obligations. These types of rights, titles, and obligations were generally laid out in the established treaties. Any court action brought by a First Nation under a Treaty would be specific to that Treaty, unlike in B.C. where the disputes, upon reaching the Supreme Court of Canada, had country-wide application.

Instead of a bias towards B.C. case law, we have included only those B.C. cases that have significance towards all Aboriginal Peoples. With the legal principles having been established through case law with its origins in B.C., other Aboriginal Peoples began to apply these principles to their historic treaties. The following three cases are significant to Aboriginal Peoples in Canada and originated outside of B.C.

R. v. Powley,[28] Supreme Court of Canada, 2003

The Powley case is the most significant decision relating to Métis people in Canada to date. Unlike Status Indians, whose identity is determined by the provisions of the *Indian Act*, there was no legal definition of who was a Métis person until this Supreme Court of Canada decision.

What began as a case over a father and son charged of unlawfully hunting a moose without a license in Ontario ended in the Supreme Court of Canada addressing whether Métis communities can possess Aboriginal rights pursuant to section 35(1) of the *Constitution Act, 1982* and—if this is the case—who can possess those rights. What came from the decision was the "Powley Test" determining the identity of individuals who are Métis.

In a unanimous decision, the Supreme Court of Canada affirmed that section 35(1) promises to the Métis recognition of their distinct existence and protects their existing collective Aboriginal rights, including the right to hunt for food.

The court held that Métis does not include all individuals with mixed Indian and European heritage. Instead, the court identified three broad factors for inclusion as a Métis person:

1. Self-identification—The individual must self-identify as a member of a Métis community and that identification must have an ongoing connection to an historic Métis community.

2. Ancestral Connection—There is no minimum blood quantum requirement, but Métis rightsholders must have some proof of an ancestral connection (by birth, adoption, or other means) to the historic Métis community whose collective rights they are exercising.

3. Community Acceptance—There must be proof of acceptance of the individual by the modern Métis community. Membership in a Métis political organization may be relevant but the membership requirements of the organization and its role in the Métis community must also be put into evidence. There must be documented proof and a fair process for community acceptance.

Mikisew Cree First Nation v. Canada (Minister of Canadian Heritage)[29]—Supreme Court of Canada, 2005

Duty to Consult in Post—Treaty Context

The Supreme Court of Canada confirmed that the duty to consult also exists in the post-treaty context in the 2005 case of *Mikisew Cree First Nation* v. *Canada* (Minister of Canadian Heritage).[30] The Court held that even though governments have a power to exercise their treaty rights, those rights are subject to a duty to consult in situations where the exercise of those treaty rights would have an adverse effect on Aboriginal treaty rights.

The Mikisew Cree First Nation objected to a proposal to re-establish a winter road through Wood Buffalo National Park for winter access from four communities in the Northwest Territories to the highway in Alberta on the grounds that it would infringe on their hunting and trapping rights under Treaty 8.

The Court found that Parks Canada had not consulted directly with the Mikisew Cree about the road, or about mitigating the impacts of the road on their treaty rights, until after important routing decisions had been made despite having provided a standard information package about the road to the Mikisew Cree, and having invited them to informational open houses along with the general public. The Crown was found to have failed to demonstrate an intention of substantially addressing Aboriginal concerns through a meaningful process of consultation.[31] The court found that because the taking of the land for the road adversely affected the Mikisew Cree's treaty right to hunt and trap, Parks Canada was required to consult with the Mikisew Cree before making important decisions.

The Court held that the impacts on the hunting and trapping rights were fairly minor, and that as a result, the lower end of the consultation spectrum was engaged. The Crown was required to provide notice to the Mikisew Cree and to engage directly with them. This engagement was to include the provision of information about the project, addressing what the Crown knew to be the Mikisew Cree's interests and what the Crown anticipated might be the potential adverse impact on those interests. The Crown was also to solicit and listen carefully to the Mikisew Cree's concerns, and attempt to minimize adverse impacts on its treaty rights.[32]

In conclusion the Court stated:

> "It is true, as the Minister argues, that there is some reciprocal onus on the Mikisew to carry their end of the consultation, to make their concerns known, to respond to the government's attempt to meet their concerns and suggestions, and to try to reach some mutually satisfactory solution. In this case, however, consultation never reached that stage. It never got off the ground.
>
> Had the consultation process gone ahead, it would not have given the Mikisew a veto over the alignment of the road. As emphasized in Haida Nation, consultation will not always lead to accommodation, and accommodation may or may not result in an agreement. There could, however, be changes in the road alignment or construction that would go a long way towards satisfying the Mikisew objections. We do not know, and the Minister cannot know in the absence of consultation, what such changes might be."[33]

R. v. Marshall; R. v. Bernard[34] — Supreme Court of Canada, 2005

Historical Treaties and "Usufructuary Rights"

Previously discussed was the significance of the *Royal Proclamation* of 1763 as a demonstration of Britain's acknowledgement that "any lands that had not been ceded to or purchased by" the Crown were reserved to "the several Nations or Tribes of Indians with whom We are connected, and who live under our protection." Many misunderstandings, disputes, and grievances about those early treaties have erupted over the years, usually arising from Aboriginal efforts to enforce the treaties. Much of the conflict has been rooted in the fundamental differences between the Aboriginal tradition of communal land rights and responsibilities and the European tradition of private land ownership.

The concept of "usufructuary right in land," or the right to use property belonging to another,[35] has been used repeatedly by the Supreme Court of Canada to explain how Aboriginal title can remain unextinguished and alive under the weight of Crown sovereignty. Usage rights are shared between the legal title holder and the usufruct. For a recent example, see Justice Lebel's Reasons for Judgment in the companion cases of *R. v. Marshall; R. v. Bernard,*[36] heard by the Supreme Court of Canada in 2005:

"Nomadic peoples and their modes of occupancy of land cannot be ignored when defining the concept of aboriginal title to land in Canada... To ignore their particular relationship to the land is to adopt the view that prior to the assertion of Crown sovereignty Canada was not occupied. Such an approach is clearly unacceptable and incongruent with the Crown's recognition that Aboriginal Peoples were in possession of the land when the Crown asserted sovereignty. Aboriginal title reflects this fact of prior use and occupation of the land together with the relationship of Aboriginal Peoples to the land and the customary laws of ownership. This aboriginal interest in the land is a burden on the Crown's underlying title.

This qualification or burden on the Crown's title has been characterized as a usufructuary right. The concept of a community usufruct over land was first discussed by this Court in *St. Catherine's Milling and Lumber Co. v The Queen* (1887), 13 S.C.R. 577. Chief Justice Ritchie used this concept to explain the relationship between Crown and aboriginal interests in land. The usufruct concept is useful because it is premised on a right of property that is divided between an owner and a usufructuary. A usufructuary title to all unsurrendered lands is understood to protect Aboriginal Peoples in the absolute use and enjoyment of their lands."

Rio Tinto v. British Columbia (Chief Inspector of Mines)[37] — Supreme Court of Canada, 2010

In the 1950s, the government of B.C. authorized the building of a dam and reservoir that altered the flow of the Nechako River without consulting the First Nations of the Carrier Sekani Tribal Council affected by this project. Excess power generated from the dam has been sold by Rio Tinto Alcan to BC Hydro under Energy Purchase Agreements ("EPAs"). Since the initial EPA in 1961 there have been regular renewals of these agreements. At the time of the 2007 EPA the First Nations asserted to the BC Utilities Commission (the "Commission") that these agreements should be subject to consultation under section 35 of the *Constitution Act, 1982*.

The Commission accepted that it had the power to consider the adequacy of consultation with Aboriginal Peoples, but found that there was no need for consultation in this case as the 2007 EPA would not adversely affect any Aboriginal interest. The adverse affects of Aboriginal interest occurred in the 1950s with the construction of the dam.

The Supreme Court of Canada held that it was within the powers of the Commission to determine whether the duty to consult had been met and continued by following the Court's ruling in *Haida Nation*'s test of when does the duty to consult arise by outlining the three elements of that test:[38]

1. The Crown must have real or constructive knowledge of a potential Aboriginal claim or right. Potential being the key; it is not proof that the claim will succeed.

2. There must be Crown conduct or a Crown decision. This conduct or decision includes government exercise of statutory powers or to decisions or conduct which have an immediate impact on lands and resources and extends to "strategic, higher-level decisions" that may have an impact on Aboriginal claims and rights.

3. There must be a possibility that the Crown conduct may affect the Aboriginal claim or right. There must be shown a causal relationship between the conduct and the potential for future adverse impacts on the claim or right. Past wrongs and speculative impacts are not sufficient.

The Court further stated that the duty to consult is confined to the adverse impacts flowing from the specific Crown proposal at issue—not to larger, adverse impacts of the projects of which it is a part.[39] Where the resource has long since been altered and the present government conduct or decision does not have any further impact on the resource, the issue is not consultation, but negotiation about compensation for the failure to have been properly consulted in the past.[40]

The Court upheld the Commission's ruling that the duty to consult did not arise because the 2007 EPA would not adversely affect any Aboriginal interest. The failure to consult on the initial project was an underlying infringement, but did not affect this 2007 EPA.

West Moberly First Nations v. British Columbia (Chief Inspector of Mines)[41] — B.C. Court of Appeal, 2011

In this case the Court of Appeal upheld an Order of the Supreme Court of British Columbia declaring that the Crown was in breach of its duties to consult and accommodate the West Moberly First Nations when granting permits to First Coal Corporation regarding its advanced exploration program.

The Court of Appeal's decision focused on two decisions of the lower court:

SPECIES-SPECIFIC RIGHT TO HUNT

1. Whether the Treaty 8 right to hunt was a general right to hunt or a species-specific right.

The West Moberly First Nations argued they had a right to hunt caribou under Treaty 8, and, more specifically, the Burnt Pine caribou herd. The court agreed, stating that the West Moberly First Nation had the species specific right to hunt the Burnt Pine caribou herd, but that this right did not detract from their general right to hunt on the traditional Treaty lands.

PAST IMPACTS EFFECT ON CONSULTATION

1. Whether the Crown, by failing to consider the cumulative impacts of past events and future events, failed to provide meaningful consultation.

The lower court considered that the past events of the coal mining operation had the cumulative effect leading to the depletion of the Burnt Pine caribou herd. The Court found that the Crown failed to provide meaningful consultation because it failed to appreciate and consider the past and future impacts to the West Moberly First Nations of the mining operations and their constitutionally protected right to hunt the Burnt Pine caribou herd.

The Court held that the *Rio Tinto* case was:

> "distinguishable from this case because in *Rio Tinto* there was a finding that the sale of excess power would have no adverse effect on the Nechako River fishery. Here, there is a link between the adverse impacts under review and the 'past wrongs.' However, *Rio Tinto* is applicable for the more general proposition that there must be a causative relationship between the proposed government conduct and the alleged threat to the species from that conduct. It is fair to say that decisions, such as those under review in this case, are not made in a vacuum. Their impact on Aboriginal rights will necessarily depend on what happened in the past and what will likely happen in the future. Here it could not be ignored that this caribou herd was fragile and vulnerable to any further incursions by development in its habitat. Thus, although past impacts were not specifically 'reeled' into the consultation process, neither could the result of past incursions into caribou habitat be ignored."[42]

While past impacts play a part in the consultation process, the Court held that this doesn't mean that the past impacts must be fully accommodated in order fulfil the requirement of accommodation. The Court held that the Crown wasn't required to rehabilitate the caribou herd to accommodate for its reduction due to the past mining activities, but rather to focus on the protection of what remains of the herd.

As the Supreme Court of Canada declined to hear an appeal brought by the Crown, these issues of past impacts on consultation and accommodation remain uncertain.

Tsilhqot'in Nation v. British Columbia
—Supreme Court of Canada, 2014[43]

The *Tsilhqot'in* decision is one of the most important the Supreme Court has decided in the last decade as it relates to Aboriginal rights and title to traditional territories and non-Treaty lands. It is a complex decision but it strengthened Aboriginal Peoples' right to their traditional territories through broader application of title than the federal or provincial governments have been willing to recognize.

The court also placed a greater onus on the Crown to ensure that proper consultation occurs under a strengthened duty to consult and accommodate with Aboriginal Peoples. By using the phrase "fiduciary duty" the court is suggesting a greater Crown obligation in consultation. Companies will need to be further aware of the risk that past authorizations (i.e. permits) that weren't provided with proper consultation may now be open to challenge from First Nations.

The court didn't establish a requirement for Aboriginal consent to Crown decisions, but it did make clear that the purpose of consultation is to try to achieve consent, not merely to go through the motions. Again the court recommending in strong terms that negotiation is the preferred method of working through these types of issues.

There are scholarly and legal discussions about whether the *Tsilhqot'in* decision changes the law or only provides for a broader application of the law around consultation and accommodation. How we view this decision is that of all the Aboriginal rights and title cases that the federal and provincial governments could have chosen to put their full resources behind, they felt this case was the strongest and had the best chance of limiting or clarifying their obligations and providing a narrower interpretation of rights to traditional territories. Instead, what occurred was another in a line of cases from the Supreme Court of Canada siding in favour of Aboriginal Peoples' broader rights to traditional territories. It confirms our belief that for greater certainty in development, governments and companies should be building better consultation and accommodation relationships with Aboriginal Peoples that would provide surety for projects instead of risking further court interpretations.

D. NEGOTIATING MODERN TREATIES AND OTHER AGREEMENTS

TREATIES ARE NEGOTIATED government-to-government contracts or agreements, used to define rights and powers and to formalize relations between governments. Indigenous Peoples in Canada have been negotiating treaties on a Nation-to-Nation basis with the federal and provincial governments of Canada, and with prior colonizing powers. Historic and numbered treaties cover much of the central corridor of Canada. Many of the early Treaties are described by the First Nations as "Peace and Friendship Treaties."

Two Examples of Modern Agreements
Since 1973, Canada has completed 20 comprehensive land claim agreements. Nine of these are termed "modern treaty agreements" because they include self-government provisions within a single, final agreement.

1. *James Bay and Northern Québec Agreement*
The *James Bay and Northern Québec Agreement* of 1975 was the first major agreement between the Crown and the Indigenous people in Canada since the numbered Treaties of the 19th and early 20th centuries. It is a very complex and comprehensive agreement, which was hard won in the courts and the media.

The *Agreement* was signed on November 11th, 1975, after four years of negotiations, court cases, and bargaining following the 1971 announcement of plans to build a system of hydroelectric dams in northern Québec, known as the James Bay Project. The affected Aboriginal Peoples exchanged their rights and territorial interests for different rights and benefits specified in the agreements.

The Cree, whose lands were at the centre of the proposed project, and the Inuit further north, agreed to joint management of wildlife with the governments of Québec and Canada. In 1978, the *Agreement* was amended after the Naskapi First Nations joined the accord through the Northeastern Québec *Agreement*. The *James Bay and Northern Québec Agreement* achieved special membership criteria (redefining Inuit and Cree status), control over local and regional governments, the creation of their own health and school boards, created measures for economic and community development, special regimes for police and justice, and environmental protection. Compensation of $225 million was divided between the Cree and Inuit and paid over 25 years. The Naskapi received $9 million (including $1,310,010 from the Government of Canada) under the *Northeastern Québec Agreement*.

The involved lands were divided into three categories: category I included 14,000 square kilometres in and around Aboriginal communities to be controlled solely by residents; category II referred to Crown land shared with the Cree (70,000 square kilometres) and the Inuit (81,600 square kilometres), exclusively as hunting, fishing, and trapping territories; and 1,000,000 square kilometres in the remaining category III, approximately two-thirds of the surface area of Québec, were designated for the exclusive rights of Aboriginal Peoples to use for traditional hunting and harvesting. For the Cree, provision was made for a minimum family-income plan for wildlife harvesting. The right to teach using native languages and in English and French was secured, and in Québec, the James Bay Native Development Corporation was established to encourage Cree economic development.

The *Agreement* was amended by seven amending *Agreements,* four additional *Agreements,* and 22 pieces of related legislation. The rights of the Aboriginal Peoples in the *Agreement* were protected by the *Constitution Act* of 1982. In 1984, the promise of self-government for the Cree was realized when Parliament enacted the *Cree-Naskapi (of Québec) Act,* the first of its kind in Canada.

2. Tsawwassen First Nation Final Agreement

Following fourteen years of negotiations, the Tsawwassen First Nation (TFN) became the first in British Columbia to sign a modern treaty negotiated through the B.C. Treaty Process. Upon ratification, the TFN stepped away from the *Indian Act* to its own Constitution which spells out the rights and responsibilities of its citizens and includes law-making powers with regard to a wide range of issues including lands and land management, social development, protection and enhancement of culture, heritage and language, taxation and financial accountability—in other words, the return to a system of self-government and autonomy to make decisions about their lives and future.

The powers of self government under the Tsawwassen treaty are limited because of the division of legislative authority within the Canadian federal system. However, they are much greater than those exercisable by a band under the *Indian Act* and include many areas in which TFN law-making authority prevails over federal or provincial law. TFN law will have the highest priority when it comes to internal matters including the use and management of First Nations assets located on First Nations lands, land use planning and development of TFN lands, citizenship in the band, adoption of children, child protection within TFN lands, teaching of language and culture, as well as kindergarten to Grade 12 education.

Stepping away from the *Indian Act* also means an end to tax exemptions. Under this treaty, personal sales tax exemptions will be phased out in eight years and income tax exemptions will be phased out in 12 years. But, at the same time, the TFN will have the right to tax and will be able to collect taxes from their members to support their government.

The TFN, which is a small urban First Nation community on the Lower Mainland of B.C., is surrounded by non-Aboriginal municipalities. Much of TFN's traditional land has been developed into cities, towns, and regional districts. The *Tsawwassen First Nation Final Agreement*, which received Royal Assent in 2008, declared 662 hectares of Crown and reserve land as Tsawwassen Lands which significantly extended the economic development opportunities available to the TFN; subsurface resources now belong to the TFN.

The *Final Agreement* also addresses a range of land and natural resources planning opportunities, including fisheries, wildlife, and migratory bird harvest and management. The TFN has the right to harvest wildlife and migratory birds for food, social and ceremonial purposes within Tsawwassen traditional territory including in national and provincial parks. Tsawwassen First Nation will also have the right to gather plants for food, social, and ceremonial purposes in specified areas.

Other Attempts at Change

In 1991, Canada created the Indian Claims Commission[1] as an independent tribunal to hear Aboriginal communities' specific land claims, arising from federal treaties and rejected by the federal government. The Commission was based on a model proposed by Aboriginal organizations.

The Government of Canada has negotiated a number of modern treaties or land claim settlements, as they are sometimes called—including the *James Bay and Northern Québec Agreement*, the *Inuvialuit Final Agreement,* and the *Nisga'a Final Agreement*. These modern treaties have been negotiated with the purpose of fulfilling Canada's constitutional obligations with Aboriginal Peoples.

In 1993, the Government of British Columbia and the Government of Canada began negotiating treaties with First Nations in British Columbia, under the supervision of the B.C. Treaty Commission, established in 1992 as an independent and nonpartisan body with authority to make recommendations, but not to compel action or to arbitrate.[2] According to the BC Treaty Commission's 2016 annual report: "65 First Nations, representing over half of all Indian Act Bands in B.C., are participating in, or have completed treaties through, the treaty negotiations process."

In 1995, the federal government affirmed its commitment to treaty-making by publishing its formal Policy Guide, *ABORIGINAL SELF-GOVERNMENT: The Government of Canada's Approach to Implementation of the Inherent Right and the Negotiation of Aboriginal Self-Government,*[3] which stated:

> "The Government of Canada recognizes the inherent right of self-government as an existing aboriginal right under section 35 of the *Constitution Act, l982*. It recognizes, as well, that the inherent right may find expression in treaties..."[4]

In May 2005, the Government of Canada and the Assembly of First Nations signed *A First Nations—Federal Crown Political Accord on the Recognition and Implementation of First Nation Governments*.[5] The declared intent and purpose of the Accord is

> "...to commit the Parties to work jointly to promote meaningful processes for recognition and implementation of section 35 rights, with First Nation governments to achieve an improved quality of life, and to support policy transformation in other areas of common interest..."

AFN National Chief at the time, Phil Fontaine, described the *Accord* as a "historic step forward for First Nations in their relationship with the federal government and an opportunity to give life to the inherent Aboriginal and treaty rights of First Nations, as recognized in section 35 of Canada's Constitution."

In November 2005, Canada's First Ministers and national Aboriginal leaders met in Kelowna, B.C., and signed a major accord called *First Ministers and National Aboriginal Leaders Strengthening Relationships and Closing the Gap*—committing federal investment of $5.1 billion over five years to closing the gap between Aboriginal Peoples and other Canadians in the areas of education, health, housing, and economic opportunity.

The Parties also signed the *First Nations Implementation Plan* declaring that:

> "… [T]he ultimate goal of this effort is to address the serious conditions that contribute to poverty among Aboriginal Peoples and to ensure that they can benefit more fully from, and contribute to, Canada's prosperity. In strengthening relationships, all parties are committed to moving forward in ways that build on the principles enshrined in the Constitution including the recognition and affirmation of Aboriginal and treaty rights."

The *Kelowna Accord*, as it was known, was a great piece of work—but was never implemented due to a change in federal government.

Self-Determination

A major objective of Aboriginal Peoples, country-wide, is for Aboriginal Peoples to gain control over who can become a member. Currently, bands are required to maintain a registry with many of the rules governing membership mandated by the *Indian Act*. As we move into the future. the desire is for communities to decide who their members are, rather than a bureaucrat in Ottawa. Self-determination is the right to decide who your people are.

Self-Reliance

Another key objective for Aboriginal Peoples is self-reliance. They want the ability to participate in the political and, more importantly, the economic mainstream, without having to rely on federal funding to meet all of their community needs. In addition to business opportunities, they also want to get into the realm of taxes, royalties, and revenue sharing on land developments—all of which are viewed as key to the self-reliance puzzle.

Self-Government

When we take a look at the day-to-day operations of a band, we see that all the actions of the band are directed in accordance with the *Indian Act*. This is a huge problem for bands and their politicians because it means that while they are elected by their people, they are accountable to Indigenous and Northern Affairs Canada (INAC). Their preference would be to change to a system where the governing leaders are elected and accountable to their people. Such models do exist and the communities with self-government agreements have done well in terms of the nation building process.

The *Indian Act* vs. Self-Determination

In recent decades there has been significant pressure to address historical *Indian Act* issues. The driving pressure comes from the combination of increasingly organized and effective political actions by various Aboriginal groups and a series of Supreme Court of Canada decisions, primarily arising out of British Columbia, that established the validity of the concepts of unextinguished Aboriginal title and Aboriginal rights of self-determination. Band chiefs and councils, other Aboriginal leaders across the country, and human rights leaders have called for increased Aboriginal autonomy from the INAC and the *Indian Act*. Taxpayers are also assessing the need for INAC with an annual federal budget to invest $8.4 billion over five years, beginning in 2016–17.

E. SELF-RELIANCE THROUGH TREATIES AND OTHER SETTLEMENTS

Aboriginal Self-Government

The term "Aboriginal self-government" is widely used in Canada—and perhaps equally widely misunderstood. "Aboriginal self-government" is often confused with more drastic and divisive concepts such as sovereignty and separation. This section has three goals: to provide clarity; to sketch some of the key issues underlying the quest for self-government by many Aboriginal Peoples; and to outline the key principles of past, present, and future negotiations toward self-government.

Is self-government the same as sovereignty?

The federal government's firm position is that all self-government structures already in place in Canada and to be negotiated in the future; will operate within the Canadian Constitution; and, be subject to Canadian sovereignty.[1]

Is self-government the same as separation?

Aboriginal self-government is about the creation of Aboriginal orders of government that will operate within the Canadian federation:

> "...as political entities through which Aboriginal people can express their distinctive identity within the context of their Canadian citizenship. Aboriginal people do not have to surrender their identity to accomplish those goals. Non-Aboriginal

Canadians cherish their identity as Newfoundlanders or Albertans, for instance, and still remain strongly committed to Canada."[2]

Is self-government the same as rights and powers?

Aboriginal self-government is about restoring rights and powers that Aboriginal Peoples in Canada have enjoyed and exercised for thousands of years, prior to European contact. It's about "the reconciliation of the pre-existence of Aboriginal societies with the sovereignty of the Crown."[3] So, the mind-set required of government negotiators, of federal and provincial politicians, and of non-Aboriginal citizens, is that the negotiation of Aboriginal self-government entails the restructuring of current forms of government to achieve the recognition and restoration of pre-existing Aboriginal rights—including the inherent right to self-government.

Why Does Self-Government Matter?

The final volume of the *Report of the Royal Commission on Aboriginal Peoples* opened with a sketch of the social, health, economic, and governance problems that confront many Aboriginal communities—in their internal management, and in their efforts to transform their relationships with other Canadian governments. The discussion then spelled out the single theme that dominates the hundreds of recommendations running through the report's five volumes:

> "Aboriginal Peoples must have room to exercise their autonomy and structure their own solutions. The pattern of debilitating and discriminatory paternalism that has characterized federal policy for the past 150 years must end. Aboriginal people cannot flourish if they are treated as wards, incapable of controlling their own destiny...
>
> " **At the heart of our recommendations is recognition that Aboriginal Peoples are peoples, that they form collectivities of unique character, and that they have a right of governmental autonomy.** Aboriginal Peoples have preserved their identities under adverse conditions. They have safeguarded their traditions during many decades when non-Aboriginal officials attempted to regulate every aspect of their lives. They are entitled to control matters important to their nations without intrusive interference. **This autonomy is not something bestowed by other governments. It is inherent in their identity as peoples. But to be fully effective, their authority must be recognized by other governments.**"[4] (emphasis added)

Community Healing and Self-Government

Most Aboriginal Peoples recognize that self-government cannot serve as a pana-cea or "silver bullet" for the deep-rooted social, health, and economic problems that plague most of Canada's Aboriginal communities. The Royal Commission on Aboriginal Peoples heard considerable testimony from Canada's Aboriginal women, many of whom stressed the need for healing in their communities:

> "Most women supported fully the move toward self-government and yet had many concerns and fears about the fulfilment of that right for Aboriginal Peoples. Why? Why do women feel such ambivalence towards the idea of self-government? The answer is clear to women...We have to change our priorities. We must have personal and community healing."[5]

The emphasis on personal and community healing is important because so many communities and their members suffer from the intergenerational effects of residential schools. The two go hand-in-hand; however, there is a strong need for individuals to go through a personal healing process and then work together with other members to bring the whole community into the process. So important is this work that some communities, when offered jobs and business development opportunities from companies, have refused those opportunities and instead asked companies for help in building healing centres. There is an emerging idea that the first steps in the treaty negotiation process should be personal and community healing followed by self-government discussion and implementation, with land issues following later.

The Costs of Self-Government (and of the Status Quo)

Everybody seems to understand that significant investment will be required to make Aboriginal self-government a widespread and successful reality in Canada. Less clearly understood are the enormous and increasing costs of leaving things as they are. Volume 5 of the *Report of the Royal Commission on Aboriginal Peoples* set out a detailed analysis of those costs, concluding that:

> "... [T]he political, social and economic conditions facing Aboriginal people impose a cost of [1996] $7.5 billion per year on them and on all Canadians; this cost is likely to rise in future, reaching $11 billion per year [by 2016]. This cost of the status quo includes losses flowing from failure to develop and use the full

economic potential of Aboriginal people and the cost of remedial action to deal with the effects of social disintegration."[6]

Guiding Principles for Negotiating Self-Government

Background

For many years, the Government of Canada refused even to entertain the concept of Aboriginal self-government. That policy mountain moved in 1973, shortly after the release of the Supreme Court of Canada's landmark decision in *Calder*.[7] Even then, however, the Government sought to narrow the interpretation and restrict the scope of Aboriginal self-government to a *legislatively* based approach: that is, to ensure that any form of self-government that might result from negotiations would come into existence as a *legislative grant* by the Parliament of Canada, and, therefore, would operate "at the pleasure of Parliament"—i.e. subject to Parliamentary amendment.

Inherent Right to Self-Government

In August 1995, the Government of Canada formally recognized the inherent right of self-government for Aboriginal Peoples in Canada by releasing its *Federal Policy Guide: Aboriginal Self-Government—The Government of Canada's Approach to Implementation of the Inherent Right and the Negotiation of Aboriginal Self-Government* (the Policy Guide)—which provides, in part:

> "The Government of Canada recognizes the inherent right of self-government as an existing Aboriginal right under section 35 of the *Constitution Act, 1982*. It recognizes, as well, that the inherent right may find expression in treaties, and in the context of the Crown's relationship with treaty First Nations. Recognition of the inherent right is based on the view that the Aboriginal Peoples of Canada have the right to govern themselves **in relation to matters that are internal to their communities, integral to their unique cultures, identities, traditions, languages and institutions, and with respect to their special relationship to their land and their resources.**"[8] (emphasis added)

In July 2000, the Supreme Court of British Columbia handed down its strongly-worded decision in *Campbell et al. v. AG B.C./AG Cda & Nisga'a Nation et al.*[9] dismissing a Constitutional challenge to the *Nisga'a Final Agreement* by the Liberal

Party of British Columbia—and, in so doing, confirming the effectiveness of the Constitutional protection of Aboriginal self-government agreements provided by section 35(1) of the *Constitution Act, 1982*:

> "That the purpose of s. 35(1) is to provide a framework within which the prior existence of Aboriginal Peoples may be reconciled with the sovereignty of the Crown can mean nothing other than that there are existing aboriginal rights which have not yet been so reconciled. In much of Canada, these rights were reconciled through the negotiation of treaties. In most of British Columbia they were not... In *Sparrow,* the Court wrote at p. 1105:
>
> > section 35(1), at the least, provides a solid Constitutional base upon which subsequent negotiations can take place. Seven years later, in *Delgamuukw,* Chief Justice Lamer referred to that passage from *Sparrow* and went on to write, at pp. 1123-4: "Ultimately, it is through negotiated settlements, with good faith and give and take on all sides,... that we will achieve..."the reconciliation of the pre-existence of aboriginal societies with the sovereignty of the Crown.
>
> "[S]ection 35(1), then, provides the solid Constitutional framework within which aboriginal rights in British Columbia may be defined by the negotiation of treaties in a manner compatible with the sovereignty of the Canadian state. I conclude that what Canada, British Columbia and the Nisga'a have achieved in the Nisga'a Final Agreement is consistent both with what the Supreme Court of Canada has encouraged, and consistent with the purpose of s. 35 of the *Constitution Act, l982.*" [10] (emphasis added)

Canadian Sovereignty

The *Policy Guide* makes it clear that all Aboriginal self-government arrangements to be negotiated with the federal government under the *Policy Guide* will remain within the Canadian Constitution and subject to Canadian sovereignty:

> "The inherent right of self-government does not include a right of sovereignty in the international law sense, and will not result in sovereign independent Aboriginal nation states. On the contrary, implementation of self-government should enhance the participation of Aboriginal Peoples in the Canadian federation, and ensure that Aboriginal Peoples and their governments do not exist in isolation, separate and apart from the rest of Canadian society."[11]

The Canadian Charter of Human Rights

It's also made clear that, as with all other governments in Canada, Aboriginal governments and institutions will be subject to the *Canadian Charter of Rights and Freedoms*:

> "The Government is committed to the principle that the *Canadian Charter of Rights and Freedoms* should bind all governments in Canada, so that Aboriginal Peoples and non-Aboriginal Canadians alike may continue to enjoy equally the rights and freedoms guaranteed by the Charter. Self-government agreements, including treaties, will, therefore, have to provide that the *Canadian Charter of Rights and Freedoms* applies to Aboriginal governments and institutions in relation to all matters within their respective jurisdictions and authorities."[12]

Jurisdiction Issues

The *Policy Guide* further defines areas that the federal government considers appropriate for Aboriginal government jurisdiction as " . . . likely extending to matters that are internal to the group, integral to its distinct Aboriginal culture, and essential to its operation as a government or institution" and goes on to specify a number of policy areas that would be appropriate subjects for negotiation:

- establishment of governing structures, internal Constitutions, elections, and leadership selection processes
- membership
- marriage
- adoption and child welfare
- Aboriginal language, culture, and religion
- education
- health
- social services
- administration/enforcement of Aboriginal laws, including the establishment of Aboriginal courts or tribunals and the creation of offences of the type normally created by local or regional governments for contravention of their laws
- policing
- property rights, including succession and estates
- land management, including: zoning; service fees; land tenure and access; and expropriation of Aboriginal land by Aboriginal governments for their own public purposes

- natural resources management
- agriculture
- hunting, fishing, and trapping on Aboriginal lands
- taxation in respect of direct taxes and property taxes of members
- transfer and management of monies and group assets
- management of public works and infrastructure
- housing
- local transportation
- licensing, regulation, and operation of businesses located on Aboriginal lands[13]

The *Policy Guide* goes on to specify a number of federal subject areas within which the federal government will be prepared to consider negotiating the transfer of "some measure" of Aboriginal jurisdiction or authority:

- divorce
- labour/training
- administration of justice issues, including matters related to the administration and enforcement of laws of other jurisdictions which might include certain criminal laws
- penitentiaries and parole
- environmental protection, assessment, and pollution prevention
- fisheries co-management
- migratory birds co-management
- gaming
- emergency preparedness[14]

No Template for Aboriginal Self-Government
Finally, the *Policy Guide* confirms that the federal government intends to pursue a much more flexible approach than in the past—rejecting the one-size-fits-all model, and proposing "… to negotiate self-government arrangements that are tailored to meet the unique needs of Aboriginal groups and are responsive to their particular political, economic, legal, historical, cultural and social circumstances."[15]

Four Examples of Self-Government Arrangements

1. The Sechelt Indian Band Self-Government Act
In 1986, B.C.'s Legislature passed *The Sechelt Indian Band Self-Government Act*,[16] providing the Sechelt Band with limited powers of self-government, including the

power to enact its own Constitution and to make laws in the areas of education, health, land use planning, local taxation, and zoning. The Sechelt Band holds fee simple title to its land, subject to limitations and conditions contained in the *Sechelt Indian Band Self-Government Act* (sections 23-25). One of the conditions is that the band holds the lands for the use and benefit of the band and its members. It should also be noted that the enabling legislation is subject to Parliamentary amendment— meaning that the Sechelt has only as much authority as Parliament delegates, which some communities regard as a relatively weak version of self-government.

2. *The Nunavut Act and Nunavut Land Claims Agreement Act*

In 1990, the government of the Northwest Territories and the Tunngavik Federation of Nunavut (now known as Nunavut Tunngavik Incorporated) signed an agreement-in-principle that confirmed their joint commitment to the division of the Northwest Territories and the creation of Nunavut. The formation of a new territory in the eastern Northwest Territories (N.W.T) resulted from a double-tracked Inuit strategy: to negotiate the broadest possible comprehensive land claims agreements with the federal government; and to participate actively in available political forums.

Inuit Members of the Legislative Assembly of the Northwest Territories collaborated with other M.L.A.s in the preparation of the 1982 plebiscite asking residents of the N.W.T. whether they would support the creation of the new territory of Nunavut in the eastern Northwest Territories. Fifty seven per cent of voters agreed.

NUNAVUT LAND CLAIMS AGREEMENT:
"...recognizes Inuit title to 350,000 square kilometres of land and provides compensation of \$580 million and a \$13 million training trust fund; it also includes provisions for joint management and resource revenue sharing...Pursuant to the *Nunavut Act*, the Nunavut Implementation Commission (NIC) was established in December, 1993...The mandate of NIC [was] to advise the three parties (federal, territorial and Inuit) on implementation questions..."[17]

3. *The Nisga'a Final Agreement*

The Nisga'a Nation's *Nisga'a Final Agreement*[18] was signed in 1998 and came into force in April 2000: conveying fee simple title to 2,000 square kilometres of the Nass Valley; creating separate jurisdictions within that territory for the Nisga'a Nation and the Nisga'a villages; and giving the Nisga'a Nation defined powers to co-manage hunting, fishing, and trapping rights in a much larger area (called the

Nass Wildlife Area). The *Nisga'a Final Agreement* and the two orders of government created by that agreement are subject to the Canada's *Charter of Rights and Freedoms*—the Nisga'a Nation has no jurisdiction to make criminal laws.

4. *The Westbank First Nation Self-Government Act*

With the signing of the *Westbank First Nation Self-Government Act* in 2005, the Westbank First Nation became a true nation with the right to govern its own affairs, and the responsibility to make decisions affecting the well-being of the community, while being held accountable to its electorate.

The Westbank First Nation Government (WFNG) provides services for residents living on Westbank First Nation lands, including those who are non-band members with residential leases on Westbank lands. The WFNG is one of the most progressive First Nation governments in Canada with a comprehensive set of laws that cover items such as land use, zoning, and animal control. It provides local government services that mirror municipal services for its residents, including law enforcement, snow removal, recreation, utilities, and public works. The *Act* covers matrimonial and property rights, language and culture, resource management and the environment, land management, and taxes.

The *Westbank First Nation Self-Government Act* also contains a provision confirming the application of the Canadian Human Rights Act to Westbank First Nation Lands and Members; the First Nation takes all necessary measures to ensure compliance of its laws and actions with Canada's international legal obligations.

F. INDIGENOUS PEOPLES: THEN AND NOW

"Indigenous Peoples[1] are all the same, right?"

Linguists refer to groups of languages that are clearly distinct, yet share enough cognate vocabulary to suggest common ancestry and origin, as language families. Canada is home to eleven distinct Indigenous language families, seven of which exist in British Columbia. Each language family is completely distinct; the specific languages within a family may be as similar as French is to Spanish and as different as Japanese is to German.

At the time of European contact, North and South America were inhabited by many diverse Indigenous Peoples, or as some would say, First Nations, representing a wide range of values, beliefs, religious views, social, political, and legal systems—and languages. Clearly defined geographic boundaries and the abundance of fish, wildlife, and natural resources allowed many Indigenous communities to develop distinct, thriving cultures, and languages. Each First Nation had its own language, culture, social structure, legal system, and political system.

Indigenous communities in Canada are made up of people from many different cultures and languages. Therefore, a generic or homogenous "Indigenous People of Canada" does not exist. That would be like referring to all people from Europe as "Europeans." When a Scot is asked, "Where did your ancestors come from?" he will answer, "Scotland." If the questioner responds, "Oh, you're European" the Scot may well be offended. It's no different in Indigenous communities. If your response to "I'm from Haida Gwaii" is "Oh, you're an Indian"—you've likely offended the person of Haida ancestry.

"What Do They Want?"

People often ask the question "What is it that Indigenous People want?" Ask a German person what Europeans want and that German person would probably be able to say what Germans want, but not what Europeans want. German interests can be something different than other European interests. Similarly, the answers as to what different Indigenous Peoples want will be as varied as the Indigenous language families and communities they come from. It is important to understand that Indigenous Peoples are as diverse as the languages and dialects they speak; even neighbouring communities may not want the same things at the same time. Therefore, your approach will need to be tailored to the particular people and community, even in places that seem close together or similar.

Are Indigenous People pro-development or pro-conservation?

I'm often asked this question in my training sessions. My answer is, "It depends." There are two considerations that come into play in evaluating a community's views on development or conservation: belief structures and socioeconomic conditions.

To begin this discussion, one must consider the history of Indigenous communities in North America. Many scholars, until recently, believed that the Indigenous Peoples who populated North America did so by way of a land bridge that stretched across the Bering Sea. The land bridge theory considers a single wave of migration from Asia at the end of the last ice age as being responsible for the population of North and South America. Mention the land bridge theory to Indigenous communities and ask them if they crossed a land bridge and their response would likely be, "No." Indigenous communities generally believe that they came to these lands through creation, not via a land bridge. This belief is supported by their respective first ancestor or creation stories.

Creation is an important belief in trying to determine if an Indigenous community is pro-development or pro-conservation. From the point of view of creation, Indigenous communities were given lands by the Creator. These lands were to be used and protected for the Indigenous communities' benefit and are required for their long-term cultural survival for the next 10,000 years and beyond. It is this ability for cultural and individual survival that Indigenous communities use as their measure of sustainability in an ideal world and suggests a pro-conservation belief.

Unfortunately, it is not an ideal world. A look at current socioeconomic conditions in Indigenous communities is the second consideration to explore. What are the key indicators showing in a community? Is there high or low unemployment? Are there high rates of suicide and violence because of a lack of economic opportunities? What health issues are affecting the Indigenous community? If a community is wrestling with poor socioeconomic conditions, and many (but not all) are, they may be more inclined to address short-term socioeconomic issues through natural resource development. Put another way, the need to survive culturally in the short-term can push Indigenous communities to be more pro-development. However, it is not development at any cost though. Indigenous communities will still weigh their development decisions against long-term cultural survival.

WORKING EFFECTIVELY TIP:
It can be very hard to achieve blanket solutions or approaches, so try not to expect them to work and consider adapting your approach to the particular People and place.

Indigenous Governance Structures in Canada: Customary and Statutory; Hereditary and Elected

Prior to European contact, many different governance structures were being used by Indigenous societies in Canada. Scholars have transcribed oral histories of matrilineal, patrilineal, and equalitarian band governments. In matrilineal communities, women held the balance of power; in patrilineal communities, men held the balance of power.

In the 1880s, section 74 was inserted into the *Indian Act*, imposing a regime for the election of band councils under a system of rules patterned after municipal law. This imposition of a foreign leadership and governance structure has been strenuously opposed over the years by many First Nations. Where such structures have been imposed, they have often contributed to breakdowns of traditional communal culture and governance, and to the destructive class divisions within communities. Over the years, many bands were able to maintain their customary and hereditary governance cultures, often running alongside or "behind" the elected band council. More recently, many bands have taken advantage of *Indian Act* amendments, allowing a return to customary and hereditary governance structures and systems.[2]

It is important to understand that many pre-contact Indigenous governance structures often included hereditary chiefs. Please note that "chief" is a European term. Traditional leaders can go by many titles, including—but not limited to—headmen/women, clan leaders, heads of villages, or groups of people; titles and roles are passed along some sort of community-driven protocol. Before commencing negotiations and before relying on band council decisions (whether elected or customary), companies and governments should prepare by learning the particular community's leadership and decision-making protocols, and should then protect themselves by confirming that the prescribed decision-making procedures were followed.

Democracy a "wonderful system: freely chosen and freely elected"

We have seen it argued that democracy suffers as a result of parallel hereditary societies,[3] such as those within many Indigenous Communities.

The "wonderful system: freely chosen and freely elected" would be great, but it isn't exactly what we have in Canada. Canada is a democracy, and its governmental form is that of a Constitutional monarchy with a federal base, which hints of hereditary governance. Canada disagreed with philosophers who took centuries of debate to arrive at the "freely chosen and freely elected" rule in favour of something that includes hereditary institutions.

So what makes democracy suffer? Does democracy suffer because people remain silent? Some would argue that democracy works because it recognizes, respects, and reconciles a variety of different views, cultures, needs, wants, and aspirations. Democracy suffers when individuals or groups of individuals in well-tailored "democratic" suits with power try to hang on to power at the expense of others and do not try to recognize, respect, and reconcile the interests of everybody in the democracy.

As with other countries, Canada has its strengths and weaknesses. One of its key strengths is that it protects individuals and groups of individuals from the tyranny of the majority, which is what we would have if we only had a democracy. The Constitutional monarchy with a federal base provides a level of protection to the minority.

Indigenous Population

Be advised that there are always at least two troublesome issues when working with statistics. The first is how statistics should be interpreted. The second issue revolves around the accuracy of the numbers. There are many different ways of defining and measuring the Indigenous population in Canada.

Identity[4]

According to the 2011 National Household Survey (NHS) 1,400,685 people self-identified as Indigenous People, and that number represents 4.3% of the Canadian population.

Out of the 1,400,685 people counted as Indigenous:

- 60.8% are First Nation
- 32.3% are Métis
- 4.2% are Inuit
- 1.9 % are other Indigenous identities
- 0.8% identify as more than one Indigenous identity

Residency by Region[5]

Out of the 1,400,685 people counted as Indigenous:

- 21.5% lived in Ontario
- 16.6% lived in B.C.
- 15.8% lived in Alberta
- 14.0% lived in Manitoba
- 11.3% lived in Saskatchewan
- 10.1% lived in Quebec
- 6.7% in Atlantic provinces
- 20.1% in Nunavut
- 1.5% in Northwest Territories
- less than 1% in the Yukon

Increasing Off-reserve and Urban Indigenous Populations[6]

49% of the population who identified themselves as Indigenous People lived in urban areas. It should also be noted that 68% of the Métis population lived in urban areas.

In 1996, the Royal Commission on Aboriginal Peoples noted that migration of Canada's Indigenous population to urban areas is steadily increasing, and that serious reserve/off-reserve inequities already exist regarding provision of services and benefits.

In 2017, that outward migration continues, as does the impact. The Royal Commission on Aboriginal Peoples cited three key issues which are still applicable 21 years later:

"First, urban Indigenous people do not receive the same level of services and benefits that First Nations people living on-reserve or Inuit living in their communities obtain from the federal government. Many status people who have moved to the city believe they are disadvantaged because they are not eligible to receive all the services to which they had access on-reserve. Métis people have little access to federal programs because the federal government has been unwilling to acknowledge its Constitutional responsibility for them.

"Second, urban Indigenous people often have difficulty gaining access to provincial programs available to other residents. Some provincial authorities operate on the principle that the federal government should take responsibility for all status Indians, regardless of where they live. Many individual service providers simply do not know what programs—federal, provincial, territorial or municipal—are available to Indigenous people.

"Third, although urban Indigenous people are eligible for federal and provincial services and programs that are available to all citizens, they would like access to culturally appropriate programs that would meet their needs more effectively."[7]

Aboriginal Youth[8]
The Aboriginal population is a significantly younger population than the rest of Canada.

- Aboriginal children aged 14 and under made up 28.0% of the total Aboriginal population and 7.0% of all children in Canada. Non-Aboriginal children aged 14 and under represented 16.5% of the total non-Aboriginal population.
- Aboriginal youth aged 15 to 24 represented 18.2% of the total Aboriginal population, and 5.9% of all youth in Canada.

Median Age[9]
The median age is the point where exactly one-half of the population is older and the other half is younger. Again, the median age statistics confirms the youthfulness of the Indigenous population. According to the 2011 NHS the median age of the Aboriginal population was "28 years; 13 years younger than the median age of 41 for the non-Aboriginal population. Inuit had a median age of 23, the youngest of the three Aboriginal groups. The median age of First Nations people was 26, followed by Métis at 31."

Fastest Growing Population[10]

Indigenous Peoples are the fastest growing segment of Canadian population. This will require concerted efforts on the part of governments and Indigenous communities to address the increased demand on housing, education, employment, and business development. The Indigenous population increased by 232,385 people, or 20.2%, between 2006 and 2011, compared with 5.2% for the non-Indigenous population

WORKING EFFECTIVELY TIP:
When working with people in general, it is very common to ask the question, "What do you do?" Given the high rates of Indigenous unemployment, this can be an awkward question for a visit to a First Nation community.

Top issues for the Aboriginal Population in Canada

A look at census figures shows interesting issues regarding Indigenous Peoples in Canada. Many more Indigenous Peoples in comparison to non-Indigenous people experience:

- Poorer health;
- Lower levels of education;
- Lower income levels;
- Higher rates of unemployment—The unemployment rate for the working-age Indigenous population is more than twice the rate for other Canadians of the same age (13% versus 6%). Nevertheless, the gap between the two populations narrowed slightly going from a difference of eight percentage points in 2006 to seven in 2011;[11]
- Higher rates of incarceration; and
- Higher rates of suicide.

These community distress issues dominate leadership thinking in Canada. Indigenous leaders and negotiators will tend to place premium value on measures that increase levels of health, education, and income in their communities, and on measures that decrease levels of unemployment, incarceration, substance abuse, and suicide.

Misconceptions

Differentiation: Aboriginal Peoples and Non-Aboriginal Peoples

Some non-Aboriginal people believe that Aboriginal Peoples, as defined by the *Indian Act*, receive "special treatment" and unfair advantages. More specifically, when we talk about the *Indian Act,* we only mean Status Indians as opposed to non-Status Indians; Inuit and Métis Peoples do not fall under the *Indian Act* and therefore do not have the same rights, benefits, and restrictions.

While there may be some benefits for Status Indians under the *Indian Act* there are many more disadvantages. Since its proclamation in 1876, the *Act* has been used to (to name a few):

- Replace traditional governing and decision-making systems with simple majority-elected, all-male band councils;
- Ban cultural events such as the Potlatch;
- Limit Aboriginal land base from vast traditional territories to small reserves;
- Eliminate economic development by prohibiting Indians to sell land, agricultural goods, or farm animals;
- Prohibit Indians from investing moneys earned by their communities;
- Prevent, until recently, Indians from voting provincially or federally;
- Limit the ability of Indians to leave the reserve (written permission from authorized by an Indian agent was required);
- Prohibit Indians from retaining a lawyer or to raise funds with the intention of hiring a lawyer;
- Remove Indian children from their homes and families to attend distant government-funded and church-run Indian Residential schools; and
- Eliminate diverse Indian identities by creating categories of "Indian-ness"—i.e., Status Indians, non-status Indians, Inuit, and Métis.

Aboriginal Peoples do, however, differentiate themselves from others in the body politic in the sense that they did not come here from anywhere. For example, if you are Gwawaenuk in the Broughton Archipelago then you are from nowhere else in the world.

Contrast this with people from other cultures who have come to Canada at whatever period in history, and you start to see the distinction. Consider a Dutch person, for example: a Dutch person coming from Holland does not have to worry about the land base, religion, political institution, artistic expression, or any other facet of Dutch culture when they make the choice to live here. Keep in mind the key distinction being that that person made the choice to immigrate to Canada—a choice Aboriginal Peoples never had.

In this sense, Aboriginal rights are human rights—or section 35 rights, as they are sometimes called by Aboriginal Peoples.

Here's a little conundrum for non-Aboriginal Canadians—ask the average Canadian "Do you support fundamental human rights as seen by the United Nations?" and most Canadians will lean towards a very strong "yes." I think they probably view human rights as one of the things they are most proud of as Canadians.

Ask the same people what they think of Aboriginal rights and many will lean towards: they should be equal, there should be one law for everybody, and sometimes they say "native equality" and not "native apartheid." It's a conundrum because, principally, they support the idea of human rights, but practically, personally, and politically, they don't. They even, on occasion, refer to Aboriginal rights aka human rights as "special treatment" which they don't think is right, fair, or equal; but, under the **United Nations Declaration on the Rights of Indigenous Peoples,**[12]Aboriginal rights include:

Article 5
Indigenous peoples have the right to maintain and strengthen their distinct political, legal, economic, social and cultural institutions, while retaining their right to participate fully, if they so choose, in the political, economic, social and cultural life of the State.

Article 11
1. Indigenous peoples have the right to practise and revitalize their cultural traditions and customs. This includes the right to maintain, protect and develop the past, present and future manifestations of their cultures, such as archaeological and historical sites, artefacts, designs, ceremonies, technologies and visual and performing arts and literature.

2. States shall provide redress through effective mechanisms, which may include restitution, developed in conjunction with indigenous peoples, with respect to their cultural, intellectual, religious and spiritual property taken without their free, prior and informed consent or in violation of their laws, traditions and customs.

Myths and Realities

There are many myths surrounding Indigenous Peoples in Canada. We call them myths because, although they do contain an element of truth, they also miss some important information. We will take a look at a number of the common myths, then provide the reality for Indigenous Peoples.

MYTH: *Indians already have ample reserve lands and resources.*

REALITY: Except for the far north (including northern Québec), where comprehensive land claims settlements have improved the situation, the present land base of Indigenous Peoples is inadequate. Lands acknowledged as Indigenous south of the sixtieth parallel (mainly reserves) make up less than one half of 1% of the Canadian land mass. Much of this land is of marginal value. In the United States (excluding Alaska)—where Indigenous people are a much smaller percentage of the total population—the comparable figure is 3%."[13]

MYTH: *Indians can do what they want with their reserve lands and resources.*

REALITY: The ultimate title to reserves lands is vested in Her Majesty. Section 28 of the *Indian Act* states: "Reserve lands are not subject to seizure under legal process." Section 32 (1) of the *Indian Act* provides:

> "A transaction of any kind whereby a band or a member thereof purports to sell, barter, exchange, give or otherwise dispose of cattle or other animals, grain or hay, whether wild or cultivated, or root crops or plants or their products from a reserve in Manitoba, Saskatchewan or Alberta, to a person other than a member of that band, is void unless the superintendent approves the transaction in writing." This has since been repealed.

Section 33 adds:

> "Every person who enters into a transaction that is void under subsection 32(1) is guilty of an offence."

The *Indian Act* is clear that Status Indians do not own property on reserves. The Minister of Indigenous and Northern Affairs Canada may issue a "Certificate of Possession" to a status Indian for a portion of reserve land, but underlying title to the land remains vested with the Crown. Thus, Indian reserve land cannot be sold except to the Crown and does not appreciate in value the same way that property held in fee simple does for other Canadians. This makes it very difficult for a status Indian to borrow funds to build a house on reserve.

The difficulty of qualifying for mortgages and loans previously noted in regards to housing also makes it extremely difficult to start businesses on reserve.

MYTH: *Indigenous People living on reserves get free housing!*

REALITY: Indigenous People can apply for social housing programs offered by the Canada Mortgage and Housing Corporation ("CMHC"). CMHC offers many programs to assist Indigenous and non-Indigenous People meet their housing needs. The programs for Indigenous People are mainly designed to give low-income families access to rental housing. Bands and First Nations that meet CMHC lending criteria apply to a bank for conventional mortgage funds to finance the social housing construction, usually with CMHC providing loan insurance. Some bands rent the property, it should be noted other bands don't even build houses for their members.

MYTH: *Indigenous Peoples don't pay taxes in Canada.*

REALITY: This misconception is proclaimed frequently, and is presented as a testament that Indigenous People in Canada don't pay taxes.

Federal tax exemptions for Status Indians have existed at least since the consolidation of the *Indian Act* in 1876, but only apply in very specific and limited conditions. Under sections 87 and 90 of the *Indian Act,* Status Indians do not pay federal or provincial taxes on their personal and real property that is on a reserve. Personal property includes goods, services, and income as defined under the Canada Customs and Revenue Agency policies. As income is considered personal property, Status Indians who work on a reserve do not pay federal or provincial taxes on their employment income. However, income earned by Inuit and Métis is not eligible for this exemption; Inuit and Métis generally do not live on reserves; income earned by Status Indians off-reserve is taxable.

The Supreme Court of Canada has concluded that the purpose of this exemption is to preserve the entitlements of Status Indians to their reserve lands and to ensure that the use of their property on their reserve lands is not eroded by taxes.

Section 87 also exempts from the federal Goods and Services Tax (GST) the goods and services bought by Status Indians at businesses located on-reserve. Goods and services purchased off-reserve by Status Indians but delivered to the reserve are also tax exempt. Most provincial sales taxes are similarly applied. In some provinces, there are certain exemptions such as automobiles which must be registered to an address on a reserve in order to be tax exempt. Again, it's a myth that Indigenous Peoples don't pay tax. Really it is only the Status Indians who don't pay taxes if the opportunity exists for them to take advantage of Section 87 exemptions. Inuit, Métis peoples, and non-status Indians pay taxes.

MYTH: *Indigenous Peoples receive free post-secondary education.*

REALITY: To say that Indigenous Peoples receive free post-secondary funding is misleading because it implies all Indigenous Peoples are eligible for funding. This is not the case. In order to create additional opportunities, their members set aside funding within their budgets to assist their members in obtaining a post-secondary education. These programs are similar to scholarship programs established by post-secondary institutions and other organizations who want to see the advancement of youth. In some of those communities with education funding, there are waiting lists too long to possibly fund all who apply. Many more communities do not have funds set aside for education funding.

Programs offered in the government-funded and church-run residential schools emphasized "Christianizing" Indians and provided training for jobs in agriculture and as domestic help—not with the goal of obtaining a post-secondary education. During this time of residential schools, access to public schools or universities for Indigenous Peoples was restricted.

MYTH: *There's no connection between Indigenous unemployment and Indigenous health and social problems.*

REALITY: Employment opportunities and rates on reserve vary considerably due to general economic circumstances in a particular region and the presence or absence of on-reserve resource bases that can generate employment. Given that incomes are low and employment prospects poor, it is not surprising that a large proportion of the Indigenous population is unemployed and lives in poverty.

Part II:
Working
Effectively
With
Indigenous
Peoples®

WE NOW MOVE into the practical side of *Working Effectively with Indigenous Peoples*®. To start, we present business case samples from the industrial and governmental perspective.

A. THE BUSINESS CASE FOR *WORKING EFFECTIVELY WITH INDIGENOUS PEOPLES®*

THESE ARE EXCITING times for Canadian businesses and organizations with interests in developing positive relationships with Indigenous Peoples and their communities. Strong winds are bringing legal and political change as well as creating new challenges and new opportunities in Indigenous relations for resource industries, for tourism, for small and medium-sized businesses, for all orders of government, and for Indigenous Peoples as well—at all levels of leadership, community development, business development, environmental protection, and more.

Many individuals and organizations are trying to figure out how to Work Effectively with Indigenous Peoples, with widely varying reasons and priorities. As we step back to look at the big picture, two primary motivators emerge: reducing downside exposure to risks and increasing upside opportunity to increase rewards.

Managing Risk Exposure
The primary motivator for individuals and organizations seeking to work more effectively with Indigenous people: improving risk management to reduce downside exposure. The risks associated with poor Indigenous relations and Indigenous community engagements are many and varied.

For industry (i.e., including housing and recreation facility development, resource extraction and processing, public utilities, and housing and recreation facility development), the risks include:

- Legal liabilities or penalties arising from deficiencies in consultation or accommodation regarding infringement of Aboriginal rights or title (whether past, current, or potential);
- Delays (and worse) in processing of applications for regulatory approval; and
- Share price devaluation, reputation damage, and customer defections resulting from negative publicity, blockades, and boycotts.

For governments (federal, provincial, and local governments) the risks include:

- Instability and cooling of investment climate and infrastructure growth, to political opposition;
- Lost tourism activity; and
- Overall damage to reputation.

In all these cases, the risks can flow directly from working ineffectively, or indirectly from being caught in the crossfire. Either way, much is at stake.

Increasing Reward Potential

The second primary motivator for improving effectiveness with Indigenous relations is to increase reward potential. The rewards can be many and varied.

For industrial companies and organizations, improved Indigenous relationships can mean:

- Greater direct access to new development opportunities;
- New indirect access through referrals and testimonials;
- Improved positioning for expansion opportunities that may manifest as a result of pending treaties; and
- Enhanced credibility with lenders and regulators.

For governments, increased rewards can be:

- Attracting new investment and employment;
- Bringing in infrastructure projects on time and on budget; and
- Appreciative electorates/constituents.

Corporate Social Responsibility

While generally not a primary motivator, the reward that comes from "doing the right thing" is nonetheless an important motivator. The term "corporate social responsibility" is overused and often misunderstood. Essentially, it's about pursuing a broader and more inclusive approach to business practices and performance measurement—placing environmental and social standards alongside, rather than beneath, financial indicators.[1] Increasingly, the business community is learning that investors and markets will recognize and reward values-based business practices.[2] In some cases, a track record demonstrating progressive social practices and inclusive Indigenous policies is a prerequisite for consideration for procurement contracts.[3] More companies, governments, and consumers are seeking social benefits in addition to financial benefits from the work and business they do, and from the goods and services they buy.

Business Case for Industrials

The business case for industrial organizations to work effectively with Indigenous Peoples has many aspects. We start our discussion by highlighting issues and scenarios framed by the lens we see as providing the clearest and most productive view of the Indigenous relations environment: **risk management**.

Risk Management

- **Past land and resource use**

  Significant legal and financial risk can be triggered by past development—by the historical footprint left behind when business changes direction or leaves in response to changing markets and times. For example, consider a reservoir built decades ago as part of a hydroelectric development. Current risk management questions would include: when was the reservoir built and did it infringe on constitutionally protected Aboriginal rights? If so, who speaks for those rights today, and with what political and financial agenda? What about the footprint issues: what magnitude of damage was caused, and what kind of compensation, court-ordered or otherwise, might have to be paid—now or over time? Some companies have since gone back and negotiated historic grievances to mitigate this type of risk.

- **Present land use and resource exploitation**

  Recent court cases have confirmed the legal responsibility of federal and provincial governments to consult meaningfully with and to accommodate Aboriginal

Peoples for potential infringement of their Aboriginal rights and title by pending development projects—whether claimed, proven in court, or agreed by treaty. If government does this well, there may be little or no risk to business. But, if government does not discharge its duties of consultation and accommodation adequately, then there are serious risks that projects will be delayed or blocked by legal challenges to permits and approvals. With those challenges can come very negative publicity and direct action campaigns that may include blockades and boycotts.

Had governments consulted meaningfully with and accommodated Aboriginal Peoples for potential infringement of their Aboriginal rights and title, there would have been significantly fewer legal challenges made by Aboriginal Peoples. Instead of considering consultation and accommodation to be the sole responsibility of government, take this as an opportunity to build relationships with the Aboriginal Peoples potentially impacted by pending development projects. Seek out opportunities to consult and accommodate whenever possible. Think and act proactively.

· **New Nation-to-Nation treaty arrangements**
In recent years, Canada has shown strong signs that it intends to continue to negotiate treaty arrangements with Aboriginal Peoples, on a wide range of issues, including land claims and self-government.[4] Section 35 (3) of the Canadian Constitution states "for greater certainty, in subsection 1, 'treaty rights' includes rights that now exist by way of land claims agreements or may be so acquired." There have been many new land claims agreements around the country in recent years—including the *James Bay and Northern Québec Agreement,* the *Inuvialuit Final Agreement,* and the *Nisga'a Final Agreement.* Industrial organizations need to follow the progress of land claims and treaty negotiations closely if they hope to ensure that their interests are heard and taken into consideration. One example would be a forestry company following the treatment of stumpage fees. In the case of the *Nisga'a Final Agreement,* eventually stumpage fees will be paid to the Nisga'a Nation for logging conducted on Nisga'a lands.

· **Indian reserve land access**
Many large industrials, such as railway companies and public utilities, need access to reserve lands for their facilities and operations. Changing Aboriginal powers, priorities, and governance can mean changes to the way business is conducted, and can mean new restrictions and opportunities regarding access to additional reserve land for future development and expansion.

- **Taxation of assets on band lands**
  Changes in governance giving more jurisdiction and control to bands over their lands have provided them with legal authority to tax developments on band lands. Industrials such as railways, utilities, and pipeline companies have been following this issue closely for a number of years. As of 2016, there were 177 First Nation communities in Canada with property tax powers.[5]

- **New Nation-to-Nation self-government arrangements**
  Aboriginal self-government negotiations can move independently of treaty or land claims talks. Industrial organizations need to follow and track negotiations when there is the potential for them to be affected by self-government agreements and the business changes they may bring.[6]

- **Legal requirements for consultation to occur on proposed new projects**
  Engineering is the easy part of building new capital projects today. The hard part is navigating the regulatory process—conducting appropriate consultations and getting the various approvals into place. The main question is: do government consultation processes that are conducted in an efficient and timely manner (from the perspectives of government and business) serve to manage risk, or do they actually create risk through their shortcomings? A process of consultation and accommodation that is fair and meaningful (from the perspective of Indigenous Peoples) can go a long way towards managing risk.

- **Maintenance of existing plant and equipment**
  Do you need to do vegetation management? Do you need staging areas such as log dump-sites or helicopter pads? If your answer is "Yes," then the requirement to consult kicks in. Again, the main question is: do the consultation processes in place manage risk, or do they create new risk through their shortcomings?

- **Regulatory requirements for consultation on new developments**
  Organizations such as the National Energy Board or Environmental Assessment Office create and oversee regulatory processes intended to avoid unjustifiable infringement of constitutionally protected rights of Aboriginal People. These processes from time to time have led to decisions that have had costly consequences for industrials. Monitoring the operations of such bodies and processes in your area of business and seeking to avoid such consequences through better consultation makes good business sense.

The second wide-angle lens we use to view possible sources for motivation to work more effectively with Indigenous Peoples is: **reward enhancement**.

Reward Enhancement

- **Continued access to lands and resources**
  Organizations that manage risk will enjoy increased rewards as they progress smoothly with development objectives and are able to maintain and gain access to lands and resources for development.

- **Address long-term employment challenges**
  Organizations are able to achieve synergies by addressing operational needs with *Working Effectively with Indigenous Peoples®* strategies. For example, workforce attrition can be addressed by targeting the Indigenous labour force, which is fuelled by Canada's youngest and fastest growing population segment. Relocation and isolation issues in the workforce can also be addressed by working with Indigenous communities, as many community members seek opportunities to work closer to home in more remote locations across Canada.

- **Take advantage of changes driven by Nation-to-Nation treaty arrangements**
  New non-Indigenous business opportunities can arise from industry restructuring driven by treaties. For example, the Nisga'a Nation negotiated hydroelectric development opportunities as part of their *Nisga'a Final Agreement* with the governments of Canada and British Columbia. The Nisga'a will likely need partners and contractors to implement those opportunities.

- **Deal with emerging Aboriginal self-government structures**
  Self-government negotiations will almost certainly continue to be a priority for Indigenous communities. Negotiations are being driven by Aboriginal Peoples themselves and by the Canadian body politic. The *Westbank First Nation Self-Government Agreement*[7] is an example of the completion of an Aboriginal self-government agreement. Those industrials whose facilities cross the lands of First Nations with self-government negotiations pending, or in progress, should follow such negotiations closely.

- **Avoid costly legal challenges**
  Being more interactive with Indigenous People and communities affords opportunities to catch misunderstandings and issues early, simplifying or even preventing costly legal challenges and project delays.

- **Protect and enhance organizational reputation**
  Working Effectively with Indigenous Peoples® can help organizations gain early and meaningful community feedback and input—keeping issues out of the public

media and fuelling word-of-mouth endorsement. In this age of globalization, companies' reputations follow them to new developments in jurisdictions throughout the world. Working effectively in one region can ensure that the discussion door is held ajar in the geographic areas of other operations.

- **Protect shareholder value**
  Share prices rise and fall by the hour following the release of good and bad news. A blockade or protest can have an immediate impact on share value should the news reach the mainstream media. We have even seen examples where Indigenous people have shown up at shareholder meetings.

- **Take advantage of social responsibility values**
  Companies are increasingly seeing the economic value of being, and being seen as, socially responsible.[8] Many new product lines are being developed with a "green" approach. Purchasing carbon credits is increasingly expected by companies whose activities can, rightly or wrongly, have a negative environmental image.

- **Meet the requirements of major financial organizations**
  Financial institutions are becoming increasingly concerned about how the business culture-related risks to which the money they lend will be exposed. Evidence of a strong track record of consistent performance in working with communities helps to alleviate such concerns.

Strategies

Many strategies are available to manage risk and increase reward by working effectively with Indigenous communities. Consider the following suggestions according to your specific needs and aspirations:

- Develop and implement engagement programs that focus on managing risk instead of blindly following government processes or policies;
- Provide training to employees to help them work effectively with Indigenous communities;
- Build capacity within Indigenous communities to help them work more effectively with you;
- Make business development with Indigenous communities a priority;
- Make workforce development with Indigenous communities a priority;
- Engage in co-management work that blends western science with traditional ecological knowledge to make decisions about land use;

- Engage in revenue sharing and co-management activities with Indigenous communities; and
- Seek to form equity position partnerships with Indigenous communities on new developments.

Business Case for Governments

As with industrial organizations, the Business Case for Governments (whether federal, provincial, territorial, or local) to work effectively with Indigenous communities can have many aspects. We have divided these aspects into two broad categories—risk management and reward enhancement. Many of these aspects are the same or similar to those outlined earlier in the Business Case for Industrials.

Risk Management

- **Government ability to grow**

  The success of First Nations and other Aboriginal Peoples on issues such as land claims and self-government will have profound impacts on those governments in close proximity to Aboriginal communities. The ability of governments to plan, grow, develop, and even expand their land base will be influenced and impacted by Aboriginal Peoples interests.

- **Past land and resource use**

  Significant legal and financial risk can be triggered by past development—by the historical footprint left behind when a development project changes direction or closes in response to changing markets and times. Did the project infringe on constitutionally protected Aboriginal rights? If so, who speaks for those rights today, and with what political and financial agenda? What magnitude of damage was caused, and what kind of compensation might have to be paid—now or over time?

- **Present land use and acquisition**

  Recent court cases have confirmed that when a federal, provincial, territorial, or even local government knows that pending development may infringe upon Aboriginal rights and title (whether claimed, proven, or agreed), that government faces legal responsibility to consult meaningfully with and to accommodate affected Aboriginal Peoples. If government does this well, there may be little or no risk. But, if government does not discharge its duties of consultation and accommodation effectively, then there are serious risks that projects will be delayed or blocked by legal challenges to permits and approvals. With those challenges can come very negative publicity, and direct action campaigns that may include blockades and boycotts.

Had governments consulted meaningfully with and accommodated Aboriginal Peoples for potential infringement of their Aboriginal rights and title, there would have been significantly fewer legal challenges made by Aboriginal Peoples. Instead of considering consultation and accommodation to be the sole responsibility of government, take this as an opportunity to build relationships with Aboriginal Peoples potentially impacted by pending development projects. Seek out opportunities to consult and accommodate whenever possible. Think and act proactively.

- **Present day treaty settlement lands**
  Many local, and perhaps even some provincial or territorial, governments believe that modern treaty settlement packages will impact them negatively, and they engage strenuously to monitor negotiations. There have also been legal proceedings—intervening to minimize those impacts. This doesn't have to be the case. A study commissioned by two B.C. government ministries and the Union of B.C. Municipalities was released in October, 2005—"emphasizing the importance for First Nations and local governments to develop positive working relationships and engage in discussions on municipal services early in the treaty process."[9]

- **Historic treaty settlement lands recognition and reconciliation**
  First Nations are continuing their long struggle for less restrictive interpretations of historic treaty settlement packages. For example, hunting and fishing interests continue to play an important role in the lives of Indigenous Peoples. Under historic treaty settlement packages, hunting and fishing rights are generally vaguely worded. In the modern reality of depressed animal and fish stocks, government reduction of Indigenous hunting and fishing allowances can result in strenuous protests and confrontations, as was experienced in Burnt Church, New Brunswick, in 2000. It remains to be seen how self-government will affect the management of treaty lands and other rights set out in the historic treaty settlement packages.

- **Self-government provisions**
  In recent years, Canada has shown strong signs that it intends to continue to negotiate treaty arrangements with Aboriginal Peoples on a wide range of issues,

including land claims and self-government. It is anticipated that new self-government arrangements will continue to emerge as treaties are negotiated or as bilateral self-government negotiations continue with the federal government. All orders of government and their administrators will want to monitor those negotiations closely, and to prepare for these emerging realities.

· **Taxation implications of land claim and self-government negotiations and changing residency realities**
Taxation by Aboriginal Peoples[10] and of Aboriginal Peoples[11] are both subjects of ongoing discussion, negotiation, and legislative reform,[12] as the percentage of non-Status and Status Indians living off-reserve continues to grow. As of 2016, there were 177 First Nation communities in Canada with property tax powers.[13] Over $70 million a year is generated in revenue from property taxes on First Nation lands, thus shifting the emphasis from personal tax exemptions to First Nations instituting property tax collection on their reserve lands.

· **Environmental assessment delays or challenges**
Some forms of development require Aboriginal consultation under environmental assessment processes or regulatory processes. It is important to understand that many conflicts occur during these processes: governments need to monitor those processes carefully.

Reward Enhancement

· **Federal programs, services, and settlements**
Provincial, territorial, and local governments will benefit from increased federal programs, services, and settlements. Programs that generate employment and business opportunities among Indigenous Peoples benefit all levels of government. An increase in federal housing services relieves the pressure on provincial, territorial, and local governments presently providing those services. Settlements of land claims and specific claims can be quite substantial, with benefits of both political and economic certainty being realized by provincial, territorial, and local government—boosting investor confidence and market activity.

· **Provincial programs, services, and settlements**
Provincial governments offer programs and services that address Indigenous issues. Both federal and local governments can indirectly benefit from such provincial or territorial programs by reducing overlapping programs and services.

- **Business-driven programs, services, and settlements**
  Big businesses have been engaging Indigenous Peoples as never before with all around benefits. Many large projects have a wide range of benefits, which may include business and workforce development, co-management, revenue sharing, payment of taxes, settlement of past grievances, and equity positions for First Nations in new developments.

- **Extraordinary events such as the Commonwealth Games and the Olympic Games**
  The formal Terms of Reference and strong community spirit underlying these extraordinary events induce governments to engage Indigenous Peoples and to show social responsibility in planning and staging. This can help to ensure that a major event is not used as a "lightning rod"[14] for protests, and is remembered as a success from many viewpoints.

- **Local government enterprise**
  Local governments have begun to see the benefits of engaging Indigenous Peoples. For example, the planned expansion of the deep sea port at Tsawwassen, B.C., involves a $47 million deal with the Tsawwassen First Nations that includes the ceding of land and commitments for future Aboriginal employment, small business opportunities, training programs, and joint-venture profit-sharing.

- **Local business supplying goods and services to local communities**
  Local governments can enhance rewards by building good relations with surrounding Indigenous communities, who will spend money in the local off-reserve business community.

  Alternatively, poor relations can mean more than just lost opportunities. Without good communication and trust already in place, a single poorly handled incident can lead to very damaging consequences. The Saddle Lake First Nation began a formal boycott of all businesses in the nearby community of St. Paul, Alberta, in 2005 after disparaging and racist comments printed in a local newspaper were attributed to a St. Paul town councillor. The store owners in St. Paul predicted that a boycott could be devastating, because as much as 60% of their business came from the 8,000 people living on the Saddle Lake reserve.

- **Develop planned projects on time**
  Working effectively with Indigenous communities can help governments to increase rewards through reducing uncertainty, defusing conflicts, and

expediting permit approvals and construction of infrastructure projects. If an Indigenous community is supportive of a development, then that's one less concern for a government agency handling the approval processes.

Strategies

Many strategies are available to manage risk and increase reward by **Working Effectively with Indigenous Peoples®**. Examine other governments' practices and performance histories in Indigenous relations and consider the following abbreviated suggestions according to your specific needs and aspirations:[15]

- Consult meaningfully and accommodate Aboriginal rights and title.
- Jointly develop regional business opportunities.
- Jointly develop regional workforce development opportunities.
- Jointly develop ways to share decision making structures.
- Jointly engage Indigenous Peoples in long-term planning processes.
- Consider and encourage revenue sharing models.

B. ABORIGINAL CONSULTATION

MOST GOVERNMENT AND business leaders have come to accept that consultation with Aboriginal Peoples is an important aspect of Canadian affairs. It was not that long ago that Aboriginal Peoples were considered and treated like the general public when it came to land and resource use decisions. The Supreme Court of Canada has led the way in the march towards change. Through a series of strong decisions issued over the past 40 years, the Court defined the following principle: when the Crown knows (or should know) of conduct that might adversely affect Aboriginal rights or title (whether claimed, proven by a court, or agreed by treaty), the Crown owes a legal duty to consult with the affected Aboriginal Peoples and to accommodate their affected interests.[1]

While the principle may now be stated simply enough, lawyers for both sides continue to seek clarification on difficult questions in the context of difficult facts: i.e., "What is meaningful consultation?"; "What is enough consultation?"; and "What is accommodation?" It is important for those about to begin consultation to avoid becoming ensnared by legal debate of these questions, which will be technical, time-consuming, and uncertain (in every sense except cost—there's no doubt that Aboriginal rights litigation will be extremely expensive).

Free, Prior, and Informed Consent and Five Key Dates for the Indigenous Peoples in Canada

In addition to the legal requirements of the Supreme Court of Canada for consultation there is now the United Nations' *Declaration on the Rights of Indigenous*

Peoples (UNDRIP) and the requirement to obtain the free, prior, and informed consent of Indigenous Peoples prior to the approval of any project affecting their land or territories and other resources, particularly in connection with the development, utilization, or exploitation of mineral, water, or other resources. Below are some of the relevant sections from the Declaration:

> Article 10."Indigenous peoples shall not be forcibly relocated from their lands and territories... without the free, prior and informed consent of the indigenous peoples concerned...";
>
> Article 11."Indigenous peoples have the right to... maintain, protect and develop the past, present and future manifestations of their cultures, such as archaeological and historical sites... [and] States shall provide redress... with respect to their cultural... property taken without their free, prior and informed consent...";
>
> Article 19."States shall consult and cooperate in good faith with the indigenous peoples concerned... in order to obtain their free, prior and informed consent before adopting and implementing legislative or administrative measures that may affect them.";
>
> Article 29."Indigenous peoples have the right to the conservation and protection of the environment and the productive capacity of their lands or territories and resources... [including] no storage or disposal of hazardous materials... in the lands or territories of indigenous peoples without their free, prior and informed consent."; and,
>
> Article 32."States shall consult and cooperate in good faith with the indigenous peoples concerned... in order to obtain their free, prior and informed consent prior to the approval of any project affecting their land or territories and other resources, particularly in connection with the development, utilization or exploitation of mineral, water or other resources."

The road to adoption of the United Nations' *Declaration on the Rights of Indigenous Peoples* (UNDRIP) has been a rocky one for Canada. Canada did finally "endorse" the declaration, but not without political pressure by Indigenous Peoples. What follows is a brief synopsis of the timeline leading to endorsement.

September 13, 2007: The General Assembly voted on the adoption of the proposal during its 61st regular session; the vote was 143 countries in favour, four against (of which Canada was one), and 11 abstaining. Canada choosing to vote against the *Declaration* was not without consequences.

September 13, 2007: The then-National Chief of the Assembly of First Nations (AFN), Phil Fontaine, gave this response to Canada's vote: *"Among many others, this declaration was endorsed by Canadian Louise Arbour, the UN High Commissioner for Human Rights. Our country, which led the way in the fight against apartheid, which played a leading role in UN declarations about the rights of women and of children, and led in the development of the 'responsibility to protect' concept, now finds itself an outlier at the UN. This is, indeed, a stain on Canada's reputation."*

December 11, 2007: The Assembly of First Nations adopted a resolution during a special Chiefs' assembly in Ottawa directing AFN National Chief Phil Fontaine to invite Presidents Hugo Chávez and Evo Morales to Canada to put pressure on the government to sign the *Declaration,* and also demanded Canada resign its membership in the United Nations Human Rights Council. "The goals of the official visit are to generate further international support for indigenous rights and social issues, establish a friendship with these visionary leaders, and establish strategic alliances with the governments of Bolivia and Venezuela," stated the resolution.

Nonetheless, work continued and gradually support for the *Declaration* from a Canadian perspective was achieved.

November 10, 2010: The National Chief of the Assembly of First Nations, Shawn Atleo stated, *"The UN Declaration compels both states and Indigenous peoples to work together in mutual partnership and respect."*

November 12, 2010: Canada officially endorsed the *Declaration: "We understand and respect the importance of this United Nations Declaration to Indigenous peoples in Canada and worldwide,"* said the Honourable John Duncan, Minister of Indian Affairs and Northern Development and Federal Interlocutor for Métis and Non-status Indians."*Canada has endorsed the Declaration to further reconcile and strengthen our relationship with Aboriginal peoples in Canada."*

May 10, 2016: the Minister of Indigenous and Northern Affairs announced Canada is now a full supporter, without qualification, of the *Declaration*.

In Canada there was, and will continue to be, much debate around the consent portion of Free, Prior, and Informed Consent. During the run up to Canada's statement of support endorsing the *Declaration* there were conversations about the legal distinction between veto and consent and whether the terms are interchangeable.

Remember that, in the *Haida* case, the Supreme Court of Canada held that Aboriginal Peoples don't have a veto and UNDRIP is silent on whether Free, Prior, and Informed Consent means a right of veto. There is a fine distinction on whether the phrase "informed consent" is interchangeable with veto. The Government of Canada has made clear it will continue to object to consent being the right of

Indigenous Peoples to veto policy and projects and prefers to focus on a continuum of consultation approach as directed by the courts. Indigenous Peoples have made it clear that they want to move forward from this debate and work towards the highest aspirational intent of Free, Prior, and Informed Consent. As stated by Ontario Regional Chief, Angus Toulouse, "The government cannot forget that First Nations have Treaty rights and the right to Free, Prior, and Informed Consent with respect to what happens on their lands."

There is no clear consensus on these terms, veto and consent, and we can expect this debate to continue over at least the short-term. Instead of spending more time and energy focusing on this distinction the parties should take heed of the pointed advice of the Supreme Court of Canada in the *Haida* decision,

> "At all stages, good faith on both sides is required. The common thread on the Crown's part must be 'the intention of substantially addressing [Aboriginal] concerns' as they are raised (*Delgamuukw* at para. 168), through a meaningful process of consultation. As for Aboriginal claimants, they must not frustrate the Crown's reasonable good faith attempts, nor should they take unreasonable positions to thwart government from making decisions or acting in cases where, despite meaningful consultation, agreement is not reached . . . Rather, what is required is a process of balancing interest, of give and take." (paras. 42-48)

Aside from determining whether an Aboriginal community has a veto in the development process, there is the practical matter of injunctive relief acting as a form of veto. If a community believes that sufficient consultation has not been provided, that community is able to access injunctive relief in the courts. Once an injunction is instituted, it has the effect of halting the development process, without quibbling over terms—effectively a form of veto.

In addition to this meaning of terms issue, there is another critical problem: the dangerous difference between whether you owe the legal duties of consultation and accommodation, or whether your project's viability is determined by the quality of that consultation and accommodation. The *Haida* case makes it clear that " **the ultimate legal responsibility for consultation and accommodation rests with the Crown. The honour of the Crown cannot be delegated.**"[2](emphasis added)

So, the duty of consultation lies with the Crown. But, here's the bigger question: "Does that mean it's a safe or wise business practice to rely on the Crown to conduct adequate and meaningful consultation?" Sometimes government achieves meaningful consultation and other times it misses the mark. Even more troublesome, if the affected Aboriginal community doesn't think that the consultation and accommodation has been adequate, negative media campaigns, blockades, and legal action can still be the result—despite what the courts may say!

How, then, do you avoid handing over the legal and economic future of your project to the government agencies responsible for Aboriginal consultation? How do you avoid legal challenges with big price tags and uncertain outcomes? On both counts, the answer is to become much more involved in the management of your organization's Aboriginal relationships. The critical insight is to see Aboriginal consultation as a risk management process not as a due diligence process to be followed.

What's the difference between consultation and engagement?

Legally, the government has the duty to consult; but sometimes governments do make project approvals without adequate consultation, which can ultimately lead to projects not moving ahead in a timely manner—even though project approval has been granted. Legal or regulatory process challenges after project approvals from governments can delay, or even result in, project approvals being sent back for more consultation. It is a risk that has to be contemplated and managed by both government and industry.

Another difference between consultation and engagement is that the Crown has the duty to consult, and not industry. This is an important distinction on who does what. Some companies name their departments Indigenous Engagement not Indigenous Consultation.

Engagement is the formal and informal way in which Aboriginal Peoples, governments, and industry can stay connected on issues of mutual interest and is generally undertaken by industry. Aboriginal People will see the two as synonymous, since from their perspective their goal is to make sure their rights are not infringed upon. Both government and industry should try hard to complement the efforts of each other.

The following diagram presents two scenarios illustrating the graduated risk zone that organizations enter into when undertaking Indigenous consultation. On the left hand side, we see that the risk greatly increases if the company allows government to take the lead on consultation. On the right side, we see a company that leads the engagement can greatly reduce the risk by engaging early and getting support from the community.

In Scenario 1, on the left side of the page, you see a large risk zone running from the time the Organization approaches Government through to the Official

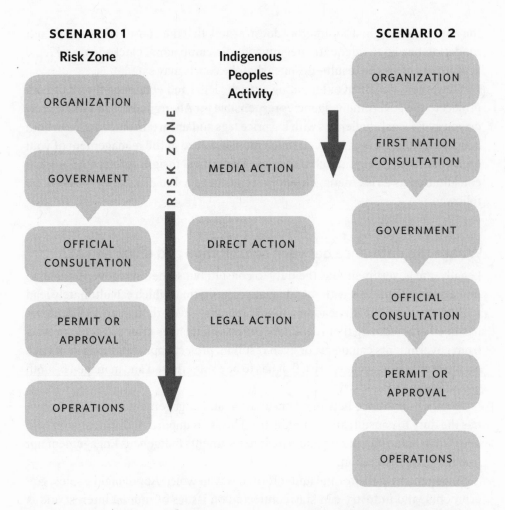

Consultation segment, to the Permit or Approval stage, and even into Operations. In this approach, by not ensuring meaningful inclusion of the local Aboriginal community in the permit or approval process, the proponents and their project face increasing risk of Indigenous Peoples Activity, and increasing potential for ensuing costs, project delays, and even project jeopardy.

In Scenario 2, on the right side of the diagram, you see an approach specifically designed to measure and mitigate risk early in the development process. Using this approach can help the Organization make better decisions about whether or not to proceed with a development project and to reduce the risk of incurring Indigenous Peoples Activity if the decision is to proceed with the project. Those decisions will be based on a better understanding of the **real** risks that they will be facing—**beyond** the legal and regulatory requirements for Aboriginal consultation as confirmed by the Supreme Court of Canada's decisions in *Haida Nation* and *Taku River Tlingit*.[3]

That means working effectively to achieve early and meaningful consultation: identifying the local Indigenous Peoples key issues, priorities, and decision-makers, and revealing the key project-related concerns that must be met to earn their support. In Scenario 2, early identification of community issues, concerns, and decision-making from a risk assessment perspective, as opposed to a positional perspective (we vs. they; who's right vs. who's wrong; and who wins vs. who loses), or a process perspective (follow the government guidelines to the letter, whatever the community says or does) can greatly decrease the risk of Indigenous Peoples Activity—and may avoid these types of disruptions altogether.

In the centre of the diagram is Indigenous Peoples Activity. This activity can include negative media campaigns, blockades, and court action. An Indigenous community is not constricted in its choice or order of use of tactics for opposing a development project. There is no requirement to begin with a negative media campaign, then move to a blockade, and only as a last resort bring court action. An Indigenous community will determine the nature and timing of its activity according to its own needs, and according to its own assessment of the situation. This makes the risk of Indigenous Peoples Activity even more difficult to predict and manage.

Negative Media

A negative media campaign is as it sounds. The First Nation or Indigenous community may engage the media in a campaign to show the less favourable aspects of an opposed development. For example, the First Nation communities against fish farming in the Broughton Archipelago (off northern Vancouver Island) offered media tours of the area, during which their reasons for opposing fish farming were presented.

The following is another example of negative media, wherein an open letter was sent to Weyerhaeuser and Abitibi Consolidated Inc. and was posted on the Grassy Narrows website (freegrassy.net):

Asubpeeschoseewagong Netum Anishinabek
Grassy Narrows, Ontario POX 1BO
Phone: (807) 925-2201
Fax: (807) 925-2649

Weyerhaeuser Company
P.O. Box 9777
Federal Way, WA 98063-9777

And

Abitibi Consolidated Inc.
Head Office
1155 Metcalfe Street, Suite 800
Montreal, Quebec
H3B-5H2

February 7, 2006

Open Letter to: Weyerhaeuser, Abitibi, Their Customers, Investors, and Bankers

Re: Cease and Desist All Logging and Industrial Resource Extraction on our Territory

For many years our people have suffered from a forced industrial invasion of our forest homeland. Our forests have sustained us for thousands of years, but industrial exploitation of these once rich forests, lakes and rivers has poisoned our waters with mercury and other toxins, nearly eliminated our ability to practice our way of life, and robbed us of economic opportunities. We are not consenting to the clear-cutting of our traditional lands, which is a continued assault on our culture, our way of life, and indeed our very existence. Leave us alone, let us use our land how we want to use it, let us feed our people how we want to feed them and then our people will become strong again.

On December 2nd, 2002, we, the people of Grassy Narrows First Nation, started a blockade in our traditional territory that still stands strong today. This letter is your final official notice that you are taking part in the destruction of our homeland against our will. You have been given fair warning that this destruction will not be tolerated. We order you to immediately cease and desist from all logging and industrial resource extraction on our territory. Terminate all logging, buying, selling, investing, financing, and profiting from the desecration of our homeland by Weyerhaeuser and Abitibi corporations and their subsidiaries. No development will occur on our territory without the full, free, prior, and informed consent of our community.

If you choose to continue engaging in, or profiting from the destruction of our homeland, know that you will face a fierce campaign against you on all fronts—in the woods, in the streets, in the market place, in your boardrooms, and in the media. We warmly invite our friends in the environmental, human rights, indigenous solidarity, faith-based, anti-poverty, anti-globalization, and all movements for social, ecological and economic justice to support our struggle, and take non-violent action in solidarity with us against the corporations that are plundering our homeland—starting with Weyerhaeuser and Abitibi. Stand strongly and proudly with us as we safeguard the basis of a bright future for all of our children and unborn generations. Take a stand with us in defence of our mother earth.

We are prepared to take all necessary actions to protect our homeland from further desecration.

The Community of Grassy Narrows.

Signed,

_____   _____
Band Council   Elders Council

_____   _____
Trappers Council   Environmental Group

_____   _____
Youth Council   Blockaders

This negative media action commenced by the people of Grassy Narrows, an Anishinabe community in northwest Ontario, has been supported by Amnesty International. Amnesty International has created a link on its webpage[4] to provide information about the Grassy Narrows' struggle, posted an open letter to then-Premier Dalton McGuinty and provided him with an online petition to respect the human rights of the people of Grassy Narrows and to ensure meaningful consultation with the community of Grassy Narrows.

Direct Action

Direct action can take many shapes and forms and can range from relatively harmless information pickets through to extremely disruptive blockades where an individual or group blocks access to a work site. In some instances, the direct action is also a negative media event where the individual or group hands out information to media. There have been many blockades across Canada, including the highly publicized blockades in Oka, Québec; Ipperwash Provincial Park and Caledonia, Ontario; and Gustafson Lake, B.C.. The longest continuous blockade is at Grassy Narrows, which began on December 2, 2002, as stated above.

Legal Action

Legal action is always available as an alternative for the Indigenous community. The courts are often called upon by Indigenous Peoples to interpret section 35 of Canada's *Constitution Act, 1982*.[5] Many lawsuits are triggered by consultation processes that some communities perceive to be inadequate and others by alleged treaty breaches. Whatever the cause and whatever the legal remedy being sought, the launch of a lawsuit on behalf of an Indigenous community threatens the Organization with expense, distraction, and delay; and, depending on the nature of the action, jeopardizes the development project itself. The main tool that Indigenous Peoples utilize here is a Judicial Review. They go to the court and request a Judicial Review of the meaningfulness and adequacy of the government consultation process. This legal maneuver can tie projects up for two to five years. Remember, they can't veto the consultative process itself, but a two to five year tie up can be effective as the project delays costs and legal fees can make it prohibitive for projects to continue. Also, market conditions and changes in government are opportunities for projects to not be pursued.

Risk, Consultation, and Accommodation Model

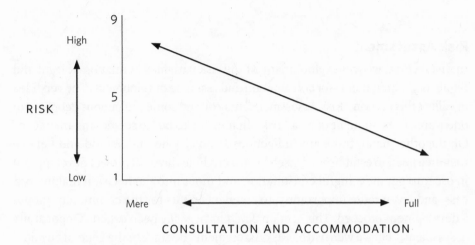

The above diagram illustrates the relationship between Risk, Consultation, and Accommodation in an Aboriginal Consultation process.

Mere Consultation and Accommodation
If the Organization engages in mere consultation with an Aboriginal community, it follows that there is little accommodation of the Aboriginal Peoples needs. Therefore, a higher level of risk of disruption by Indigenous Peoples Activity is being assumed by the Organization.

Full Consultation and Accommodation
On the other hand, if there is full consultation, it also follows that the Aboriginal Peoples needs are more likely being accommodated and less risk of disruption is being assumed by the Organization.

Consultation Policy
A consultation challenge lies in the potential for differences in perspective regarding the ingredients of "meaningful consultation." It is prudent to confirm at an early stage all players' perceptions of the applicable consultation policy (usually written by federal and/or provincial/territorial government officials). If there is a large gap between the governmental and Aboriginal expectations for the consultation

process, then you can expect a higher level of risk to be assumed by the proponent Organization.

Risk Assessment

In this section, we will explore many of the risk variables in relation to legal and regulatory requirements for consultation and resource development. The very idea of calling this section "Risk Assessment" may offend some Indigenous Peoples. No one wants to be thought of as a "risk" that needs to be "assessed and managed." On the other hand, there are Indigenous Peoples who understand and believe that they need to establish themselves as a credible threat in project development in order to get meaningful consultation and input into the decision making process; and, even more importantly, to receive benefits for the community should a development proceed. This section could have easily been called "Opportunity Assessment," but we went with "Risk Assessment" because of the general business understanding and acceptance of the concept of that term.

The following Risk Assessment framework has been designed primarily as a tool to be used by investors and financiers in assessing the risks associated with specific projects. The assessment tool has been developed from the perspective of investment. However, government and business representatives also can use it to assess risks, and to identify actions they can take to mitigate those risks on behalf of developers, thereby promoting economic certainty. Indigenous governments can also use the tool to conduct an effective self-assessment—determining how others may see their community(ies). Indigenous Peoples could use "legal challenges, such as judicial reviews or rights and title claims."

The assessment tool takes into account that Indigenous rights are held communally, not individually. Companies can do well if they involve broader communities in the decision-making process and look beyond the band leadership.

Because this assessment process identifies Indigenous communities that lack the capacity to protect their rights and title, and those that have the capacity to effectively defend their rights and title, some governments and companies might be tempted to roll over weaker communities—consulting only those that present a "credible" threat. That would be a dangerous misuse of this tool. Rolling over a weaker community is not only socially irresponsible, but it can be economically risky as well. Proceeding without consultation may inspire that weaker community to turn itself into a credible threat after all. Such a threatening metamorphosis could arise well into the lifespan of the project: after significant monetary or time investment—triggering significant new expense and risk. One must keep in mind that the risk of blockades and negative media campaigns always exist—from commencement through completion of a project.

The risk assessment scale is rated from 1 to 9. "1" meaning a low risk and "9" meaning a high risk. Below the scale are low, medium, and high risk examples for each variable. The assessor is required to determine where the particular situation lies on the risk scale. Each variable can then be plotted on a graph similar to the diagram of the Risk, Consultation, and Accommodation Model examined earlier, providing the assessor with a snapshot of the risk variable for the particular situation.

BLOCKADE								
1	2	3	4	5	6	7	8	9

1 Blockades have never been an issue
5 The community has threatened to blockade
9 The community has blockaded in the past

The blockade represents one of the tools that Indigenous Peoples use when trying to get governments and companies to take action on certain issues. Blockades have been used successfully by both large and small communities to draw attention and action to certain issues. Blockades can take the form of armed standoffs, road closures, or information checkpoints, lasting a day or going on for years.

BAND COUNCIL ELECTION								
1	2	3	4	5	6	7	8	9

1 There is a band council election in 2 or more years
5 There is a band council election in 6 to 9 months
9 There is a band council election in 3 months or less

Organizations need to understand that when Indigenous communities change governments, dramatic changes in the business climate can soon follow.

Indigenous communities are not unique to change in governments. This is the same for non-Indigenous communities (i.e., local, provincial, territorial, and federal governments). In Canada, many band elections take place on a two year cycle. Just as an Organization may have strategies in place for the change of a federal, provincial, or territorial government, it is just as important for Organizations to be aware of potential changes in Indigenous governments and have strategies in place to limit the impact of those changes on operations.

DECISION MAKERS								
1	2	3	4	5	6	7	8	9

1 Consult widely through elected council, hereditary chiefs, Elders, and community
5 Try to reach broader community
9 Only deal with the chief and council

Indigenous rights and title are held collectively by a community. Some Indigenous Peoples require broad consensus for all decisions that affect collective community interests. In other communities, such decisions are made by the elected chief and council; in still others, the hereditary chief and traditional Elders hold that authority. This portion of the assessment requires consideration of tough questions such as: "Are the chief and council authorized to make decisions about rights and title without community involvement?"; "Is it up to the hereditary or traditional system to make those decisions about rights and title?"; and, "Is the whole community required to be involved in the decision making process?" Finding the answers to these questions and developing appropriate response strategies should lead to a smoother path toward certainty.

NEGATIVE MEDIA CAMPAIGN								
1	2	3	4	5	6	7	8	9

1 Community has never threatened a negative media campaign
5 Community has threatened a negative media campaign
9 Community has conducted a negative media campaign

Negative media campaigns are always an option for communities—even those with limited resources. Media campaigns don't take much to organize and can be highly effective at drawing attention to issues. The main question to be asked here is: "If our organization commits resources to an activity that the community does not support, what is the propensity for the community to engage in a negative media campaign?"

LEGAL ACTION								
1	2	3	4	5	6	7	8	9

1 Community has never threatened legal action
5 Community has now or in the past threatened legal action
9 Community has now or in the past commenced legal action

For decades, Indigenous communities in Canada have made very effective use of legal action to pursue their rights and grievances. Even smaller communities with limited resources are adept fundraisers by appealing to supporters in Canada, the United States, and other parts of the world to help them launch court actions against governments and businesses. The question is, "If our organization commits resources to an activity that the community does not support, what is the propensity for the community to engage in legal action?"

COMMUNITY FINANCIAL RESOURCES								
1	2	3	4	5	6	7	8	9

1 Smaller size membership with only federal funding revenue
5 Moderate size membership relying on federal and provincial funding revenue
9 Large membership with a blend of federal, provincial and independent
   sources of revenue

A community's financial resources can be a determining factor for the adequacy of its participation in consultation and risk management. Key questions include: "Does the community have access to the technical capacity needed to evaluate our proposed project?"; "Does the community have strong support from its financial institution?"; and "Does the community have strong fundraising potential?" From a lender's perspective, a community without adequate resources to fund proper technical analysis and legal advice represents risk. It leaves the door open to sharp dealings by governments or companies, and then to Indigenous Peoples Activity. Lenders should be aware of these potential sharp-dealing scenarios: timely loan repayments hang in the balance as project permits, schedules, and budgets are placed in jeopardy.

ORGANIZATION'S APPROACH TO CONSULTATION POLICY								
1	2	3	4	5	6	7	8	9

1 Timeline's not an issue; community approval is secured before permit application is filed; community is involved in planning and will benefit from development activities

5 Send letter; make follow up calls and visits, if appropriate; address issues and concerns raised

9 Send letter, wait 30 days; if no response, proceed to permit application

There can be big differences between what federal, provincial, and territorial governments and Indigenous Peoples consider a good consultation policy. Indigenous consultation policies are usually written by government officials and tend to focus more on process-management issues such as jurisdiction, due diligence protocol, timelines, and damage control and less on relationship-building issues such as recognition, values, priorities, and consensus. Recent Supreme Court of Canada decisions have stressed the importance of understanding and honouring the underlying purpose of the Crown duty of consultation. The following passages from the leading case of *Haida Nation* are instructive:

Source of the Duty

"The government's duty to consult with Aboriginal Peoples and accommodate their interests is grounded in the honour of the Crown. The honour of the Crown is always at stake in its dealing with Aboriginal Peoples... The historical roots of the principle of the honour of the Crown suggest that it must be understood generously in order to reflect the underlying realities from which it stems. In all its dealings with Aboriginal Peoples, from the assertion of sovereignty to the resolution of claims and the implementation of treaties, the Crown must act honourably. **Nothing less is required if we are to achieve "the reconciliation of the pre-existence of Aboriginal societies with the sovereignty of the Crown."** (*Delgamuukw* at para. 186)[6] (emphasis added)

When the Duty to Consult Arises

"[T]he duty to consult and accommodate is part of the process of fair dealing and reconciliation that begins with the assertion of sovereignty and continues beyond formal claims resolution. Reconciliation is not a final legal remedy in the usual sense. Rather, it is a process flowing from the rights guaranteed by s. 35(1) of the *Constitution Act, 1982*. This process of reconciliation flows from the Crown's assertion of sovereignty over an Aboriginal people and *de facto* control of land and resources that were formerly in the control of that people ... To limit reconciliation to the post-proof sphere risks treating reconciliation as a distant legalistic goal, devoid of the 'meaningful content' mandated by the 'solemn commitment' made by the Crown in recognizing and affirming Aboriginal rights and title ... It also risks unfortunate consequences. When the distant goal of proof is finally reached, the Aboriginal Peoples may find their land and resources changed and denuded. This is not reconciliation. Nor is it honourable."[7]

While this process of reconciliation and honour may be a fine moral and legal starting point, let's cut to the practical problem:

> **"But, when precisely does a duty to consult arise? The foundation of the duty in the Crown's honour and the goal of reconciliation, suggest that the duty arises when the Crown has knowledge, real or constructive, of the potential existence of the Aboriginal right or title and contemplates conduct that might adversely affect it."**[8] (emphasis added)

From the investor/lender perspective, important questions to ask include: "Has the Organization and/or government applied consultation policy as a means to get to permitting, or as an element of a relationship-building strategy?"; "Is the risk of Indigenous Peoples Activity being managed by the current consultation policy and practice?"; and, "If the risk isn't managed, are there perhaps better lending opportunities elsewhere?"

The timeline issue raises two key questions for an investor or lender to consider: "Did the Organization insist on strict Indigenous consultation timelines?" and, if so,

"How did the Indigenous Peoples respond to those timelines?" Some timelines are so short that it would be tough even for a community with a great amount of capacity to meet them. Some Indigenous communities will be insulted and alienated by the tight timeline approach; it would be dangerous to interpret their non-response as acquiescence.

ORGANIZATION'S TEAM								
1	2	3	4	5	6	7	8	9

1 Team agrees to do what is necessary in terms of capacity building, job and business development, management, etc., to ensure support for project

5 Team still struggling with concepts of equality but can accept other alternatives ways of doing things

9 Team believes that Indigenous Peoples should be treated "equal to all Canadians"

The core challenges for an Organization are often rooted in the Indigenous perspectives of its Team members. If you ever hear an Organization Team member asking, "Why do I have to treat them differently?" or "Why can't we treat them like everyone else?"—you should know there is a high likelihood that things could go wrong with the project. This type of comment should raise serious "red flags" about this team member's ability to perform well in this environment. Such questions completely ignore constitutionally protected Indigenous rights, which form the basis for many landmark court cases. You could ask an Organization Team member a simple question such as, "What are your thoughts on fishing and hunting rights?" The response will give you important clues about the degree of interest this Team member has in consulting and accommodating Indigenous communities.

ORGANIZATION'S VIEWS								
1	2	3	4	5	6	7	8	9

1 Organization's action meets or exceeds consultation policy and is supported by senior executives and throughout the organization

5 Organization has an Indigenous relations policy, but shows little or no action to support it

9 No Indigenous relations policy; believes consultation is a government issue

Does the Organization have an Indigenous relations policy and does it seek ways to include Indigenous neighbours in its decision-making processes and business opportunities? There are companies that have Indigenous relations policies, but provide little in the way of resources or agreements to actualize them. Reports can seem positive about the nature of relationships, but the real test will be for the lender or investor to verify the true strength of the relationship with the particular Indigenous community. A lender or investor should be aware that an Organization lacking an Indigenous relations policy likely also lacks experience in working with Indigenous communities. This lack of experience can leave the door open to many issues that will need to be resolved before a project can proceed in a suggested timeline.

INDIGENOUS COMMUNITY MEMBERSHIP								
1	2	3	4	5	6	7	8	9

1 Community members include lawyers, doctors, teachers, trades, etc. The community has friends with extensive business experience in the global community and government. Community members conduct the community's affairs, with little or no reliance on consultants

5 Community members have some bench strength, less reliance on consultants

9 Community members have little bench strength—no lawyers or accountants, and the community relies heavily on outside consultants

This is primarily a question of human resource capacity within a community. A shortage of capacity at the community level and heavy reliance on consultants may lead to poor decisions by community leaders, and to withhold community support for those decisions. Communities are not afraid to revisit decisions that can affect their long-term survival as a community, even years into a project. The investor or lender will want to have a snapshot of human resources capacity within the community. Good internal capacity leads to better decisions, greater community stability, and longer-term business certainty. Poor community capacity can lead to poor decisions and perhaps to the need to revisit past decisions.

CAPACITY BUILDING								
1	2	3	4	5	6	7	8	9

1 Organization makes resources available to the community for legal analysis, studies, participation at meetings, hiring a community liaison person, etc.
5 Some resources are made available for studies
9 No resources are dedicated by the Organization or government for community capacity building

One of the biggest challenges of Indigenous consultation lies in the chronic problem of overloaded Indigenous community capacity. Communities can receive hundreds of requests for consultation in a very short period of time as business and government attempt to fulfill legal and regulatory requirements for consultation.[9] Simply put, if they don't have the people or resources, they lack the capacity to deal with the requests. Organizations can improve their management of consultation risks by supporting community capacity-building.

AGENDA COMPETITION								
1	2	3	4	5	6	7	8	9

1 There are only one or two other Organizations and governments competing for space and place on the community agenda
5 There are a few other Organizations and agencies competing for placement on the community agenda
9 There are many other Organizations and government agencies competing for placement on the community agenda

Another challenge of Indigenous consultation is what can be called "agenda competition." In order to understand agenda competition, you first need to appreciate some of the short- and long-term challenges facing Indigenous leaders.

The first agenda issue to consider is that a band chief and council have the mandate to look after their members, and to manage the day-to-day interests of the band and its reserve land. Daily activities of a band chief and council may include, but are not limited to, household repairs, negotiating or renewing right of ways on reserve, looking after housing, administration of educational and health programs, maintenance of band membership lists, and other duties.

Other major areas of concern for chiefs and council are complex, long-term issues: the resolution of land claims, recognition of treaty rights, and the pursuit of self-government. While virtually all Indigenous communities will have these matters on their agendas, each will have its own timetable and priorities, and each will have its own political and capacity realities. Some bands may choose to resolve these issues through treaty negotiations, others may look to the courts, and still others may focus on negotiating interim measures and immediate business development. It is important to recognize that these activities consume a great deal of leadership time and energy.

COMMUNITY BENEFITS FROM PROJECT								
1	2	3	4	5	6	7	8	9

1   Co-management and revenue/resource sharing
5   Business and workforce development
9   Little or no discussion of community benefits

A big tell-tale for *Working Effectively with Indigenous Peoples*® is the issue of "project benefits." Is the Indigenous community benefiting from the project? Are opportunities for jobs, business development, co-management, and revenue-sharing flowing through to the community? It would be hard to understand how an Indigenous community would support development of its ancestral lands without receiving any benefit from that development—especially given the difficult socio-economic circumstances of most communities. The current middle of the road route focuses on business and workforce development, but the future will likely see more co-management and revenue-sharing.

RETURN ON INVESTMENT								
1	2	3	4	5	6	7	8	9

1 Organization understands that every dollar spent on working with communities shows a positive return on investment

5 Organization is starting to see that working effectively provides value but is not looking at it from a return on investment perspective

9 Organization does not see a return on investment for working with Indigenous communities

The toughest questions we get about *Working Effectively with Indigenous Peoples®* revolve around money. Business people often ask, "Where is the money going to come from to fund Indigenous jobs, business development, capacity-building, and consultation?" Many business leaders still see developing relations as an unplanned expense that shouldn't be their responsibility.

Understanding Consultation from a Regulatory Perspective

The landscape for companies involved in the extraction and development of natural resources has changed dramatically in the last few decades with respect to regulation. As we have moved from the pioneer days of no-to-low regulation to today with more regulation than ever, one of the primary issues currently influencing the natural resource sector, along with environmental protection, are Aboriginal issues such as land claims and self government.

We have seen everything from blockades, negative media campaigns, and legal action—all of which have far-reaching consequences for the resource sector. Part of the response from government has been to introduce or change regulation designed to address Aboriginal Peoples and their cultures.

Before discussing balancing regulation with culture, I think it is important to understand what the word "culture" means. The Merriam-Webster dictionary describes part of the definition of culture as "the integrated pattern of human knowledge, belief, and behaviour that depends upon the capacity for learning and transmitting knowledge to succeeding generations and the customary beliefs, social forms, and material traits of a racial, religious, or social group."

The problem with this definition of culture is that it comes across as a non-threatening concept. It makes people think that culture is language, dancing, and crafts. One might think, "Why should I, or the government for that matter, be worried about culture? We live in a society that allows people to be who they are by providing freedom of religion and all manner of other freedoms."

This in turn can make resource development companies think: It will be easy to balance their culture with regulation and the regulators will be happy with me. I will be granted my permit, and things will proceed as planned." However, this is not the case and is a total underestimation of what we are actually dealing with.

To get to the root of what we are dealing with, we need an equation. Culture equals something? Culture in the case of Aboriginal Peoples equals constitutionally protected legal rights. These legal rights are the leverage that Aboriginal Peoples have to protect their cultures. Below is section 35 of the Constitution of Canada. Be sure to pay particular attention to section 35(1).

RIGHTS OF THE ABORIGINAL PEOPLES OF CANADA
Recognition of existing aboriginal and treaty rights

35. (1) The existing aboriginal and treaty rights of the aboriginal peoples of Canada are hereby recognized and affirmed.

Definition of "Aboriginal Peoples of Canada"

35. (2) In this Act, "aboriginal peoples of Canada" includes the Indian, Inuit, and Métis peoples of Canada.

Land claims agreements

35. (3) For greater certainty, in subsection (1) "treaty rights" includes rights that now exist by way of land claims agreements or may be so acquired.

Aboriginal and treaty rights are guaranteed equally to both sexes

35. (4) Notwithstanding any other provision of this Act, the aboriginal and treaty rights referred to in subsection (1) are guaranteed equally to male and female persons. (96)

There is a lot of meaty stuff in section 35, but—from the perspective of regulation and culture—section 35(1) says it all. It states that "the existing aboriginal and treaty rights of the aboriginal peoples in Canada are recognized and affirmed."

What does this mean? It means that, from a federal, provincial, and territorial government perspective, governments have to recognize and affirm rights and not take them away through regulation or subsequent activity or activities. There is a legal principle from the 1990 *Sparrow* decision that states that any proposed government regulation that infringes on the exercise of Aboriginal rights must be constitutionally justified.

Further, the *Delgamuukw* Supreme Court decision of December 1997 stated that Aboriginal rights and title exist and governments must design regulations to avoid infringing on constitutionally protected rights. Keep in mind that from the court's perspective, the discussion about whether Aboriginal rights exist is over and closed. The Supreme Court of Canada has required the government to shift their focus to a process of defining those existing Aboriginal and treaty rights through regulation, consultation, or treaty and reconciliation negotiations.

It follows then that Aboriginal Peoples for the most part look at the world through section 35 glasses and ask themselves a simple question—"Does this regulation and subsequent activity infringe on the exercise of our constitutionally protected rights?" If the regulation or subsequent activity does infringe, then they have legal remedy not available to other peoples or their cultures.

One potential remedy is to go to court and seek judicial reviews challenging permits usually on the basis of lack of consultation. Such judicial reviews can tie projects up for lengthy periods of time incurring huge project delay costs, as well as associated legal fees.

What, then, can you do to balance culture with regulation? Change the focus from culture to constitutionally protected legal rights, and do whatever it takes to avoid infringing on constitutionally protected rights. The key is to engage with Aboriginal Peoples early and often, avoid infringing, seek accommodation, and don't assume that by simply fulfilling legal and regulatory requirements that projects will proceed as you wish. Many have tried this approach, and many have failed.

A Case Study: Private Land, Environmental Assessment, and Consultation

Consultation with Aboriginal communities is an issue of emerging importance to local governments. Where planned developments or activities may infringe on Aboriginal rights, it may not be an answer simply to place the developments or activities on privately held lands.

The Greater Vancouver Regional District (GVRD) proposed to develop a major landfill near the town of Ashcroft, B.C., about 350 kilometres north of Vancouver. In 2000, the GVRD purchased fee simple title to a ranch property—believing that as non-Crown land, the property was not subject to Aboriginal land claims or consultation policies. Environmental groups and the local First Nations raised concerns that alternatives to the landfill had not been considered, and that the significant environmental and health risks associated with the proposed "mega" landfill were not being adequately addressed. In June 2005, B.C.'s Minister of Sustainable Resource Management suspended the Environmental Assessment process, directed the GVRD to complete its Solid Waste Management Plan, and to "look at all possible alternatives, [including] alternative sites, and alternative approaches to waste reduction."

The Ashcroft First Nation has said that it will go to court to protect its source of water from the landfill. Robert Pasco, Chairman of the Nlaka'pamux Nation Tribal Council, made the point bluntly."Indigenous communities are tired of being dumped on—now literally. The Ashcroft proposal will not succeed," he vowed.

The GVRD's review of alternatives and completion of its Solid Waste Management was expected to take at least 18 months—running perilously close to the 2008 deadline for closure of its existing Cache Creek landfill facility. It is interesting to consider how differently this situation might have unfolded had local First Nations been consulted regarding their concerns for the proposed Ashcroft Ranch Landfill—meaningfully, and at an early stage of the planning process.

C. RESPECT: A PATH TOWARD *WORKING EFFECTIVELY WITH INDIGENOUS PEOPLES*®

HOW DO WE work effectively with indigenous peoples? Is there one process that we can use that will work in every situation? The short answer is, "No." The process used in any given situation will change depending on the community or communities involved, and depending on the various policies, and legal, cultural, and regional considerations on the table.

Many prominent national Indigenous leaders have commented that any effective Indigenous relations process should be designed to address the three Rs— **Recognition**, **Respect**, and **Reconciliation**. "Recognition" means to recognize constitutionally protected Aboriginal rights. "Respect" means to address the uniqueness of individual Indigenous Peoples, their cultures, and their constitutionally protected rights. Lastly, "Reconciliation" means to restore harmony between Indigenous and non-Indigenous people.

RESPECT
From the concept of the three Rs, **Indigenous Corporate Training Inc.** developed a training model called **RESPECT** which is designed to provide guidance to individuals and organizations seeking to build effective relationships with Indigenous People.

RESPECT stands for: **R** esearch
E Evaluate
S trategize
P resent
E valuate
C ustomize
T ransform

THE MODEL BELOW provides a visual tool that depicts **RESPECT** as a continuous process of learning, development, and evolution. We present **RESPECT** not as a firm protocol for behaviour, but rather as a principled approach to relationship-building, which we see as the key to *Working Effectively with Indigenous Peoples®*.

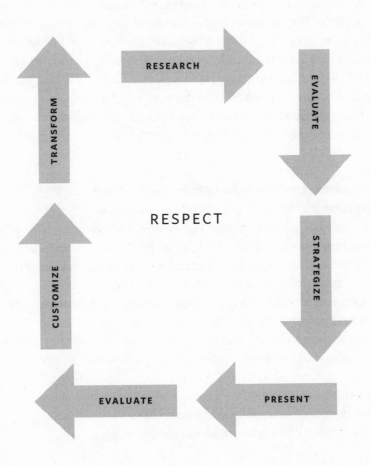

Research

A critical component of working effectively with Indigenous communities is "Research." We use the term "Indigenous Peoples" to indicate the uniqueness and diversity of the various First Nation, Inuit, and Métis Peoples[1] who live in Canada, with their different histories, traditions, values, worldviews, beliefs, and aspirations. We use the term "Aboriginal Peoples" to indicate the collective group of people who hold various rights and obligations under provisions of the *Indian Act* and the Canadian *Constitution Act, 1982*, to which the general public are not subject. These differences create a business context similar to doing business in another country. The successful international business person would not go to another country to do business without researching legal and cultural differences, and without considering their impact on business processes and practices.

Research is not limited to studying the community with whom you are considering doing business or developing a working relationship. You need to start by researching within. First, you must determine where you, your colleagues, and your organization stand on working with Indigenous People, and on Indigenous issues. Prior to embarking on a relationship-building strategy, conduct the following assessment to determine your organization's level of understanding and support for Indigenous People and issues. The answers should inform you regarding the amount and focus of internal work required before your organization embarks on a plan to build effective working relationships with Indigenous Peoples.

YOU:
- ☐ Are you comfortable working with Indigenous People?
- ☐ Are you comfortable working with Indigenous issues?
- ☐ Have you worked with Indigenous Peoples and communities in the past?
- ☐ Are you currently working with Indigenous Peoples and communities?
- ☐ Would you like to see Indigenous land claims resolved sooner rather than later?
- ☐ Do you support a municipal model of Indigenous self-government?
- ☐ Do you support a model of self-government that includes broader powers?
- ☐ Do you have personal contacts for Indigenous advice?
- ☐ Do you have time to learn about Indigenous Peoples and Indigenous issues?
- ☐ Are you willing to give up other activities to make time for Indigenous learning?

YOUR COLLEAGUES:
- ☐ Are they comfortable working with Indigenous Peoples?
- ☐ Are they comfortable working with Indigenous issues?

☐ Have they worked with Indigenous communities in the past?
☐ Are they currently working with Indigenous communities?
☐ Would they like to see land claims resolved sooner rather than later?
☐ Do they support a municipal model of self-government?
☐ Do they believe in native equality, not native apartheid?
☐ Do they believe they have "special" fishing and hunting rights?
☐ Do they have time to learn about Indigenous Peoples and Indigenous issues?
☐ Are they willing to give up other activities to make time for Indigenous learning?

YOUR ORGANIZATION:

☐ Is your organization comfortable working with Indigenous Peoples?
☐ Is your organization comfortable working with Indigenous issues?
☐ Has your organization worked with Indigenous communities in the past?
☐ Is your organization currently working with Indigenous communities?
☐ Does your organization publicly support the idea of respect, recognition and reconciliation of constitutionally protected Aboriginal rights?
☐ Does your organization publicly support the inherent right of Indigenous self-government?
☐ Will your organization commit time to learn about Indigenous Peoples and Indigenous issues?
☐ Is your organization willing to give up other activities to make time for Indigenous learning?
☐ Can your organization "do what it takes" to get the job done?
☐ Will your organization commit funds to capacity-building for Indigenous Peoples?
☐ Does your organization have a formal Indigenous relations policy?
☐ If so, will that policy give you leverage when working internally to promote Indigenous relations?
☐ Can and will your organization extend timelines to accommodate working with Indigenous Peoples?
☐ Does your organization understand that its objectives and Indigenous community objectives won't always mesh?

Research should also be conducted on the Indigenous Peoples with whom you may develop a relationship. Ideally, that research should be performed before you and your organization begin working in the community. But, better late than never!

The following is a quick checklist to get you started in your research. Following the checklist are more detailed research topics for further consideration.

CULTURAL BACKGROUND INFORMATION:

☐ Community cultural centres
☐ Provincial museums
☐ Books on communities
☐ Books by community authors
☐ Traditional use studies
☐ Government websites (federal and provincial)
☐ Community websites
☐ Other public submissions (i.e., regulatory submissions)

PEOPLE YOU SHOULD CONSIDER TALKING TO:

☐ Government representatives who have worked with the community or communities in question; federal and provincial at a minimum.
☐ Consultants
☐ Lawyers
☐ Economic development officers
☐ Contacts from the specific Indigenous community(ies)

INFORMATION TO LOOK FOR:

☐ Community profiles and statistics
☐ Fishing, hunting, and gathering activities
☐ Spiritual practices
☐ Custom, elected, or majority elected leadership
☐ Tribal council or Treaty offices affiliations
☐ Other political affiliations (i.e., Assembly of First Nations)
☐ Decision-making structures
☐ Staff directories as a way to determine who to talk to
☐ Community priorities
☐ Date of the next band election
☐ Questions they will ask you
☐ Media stories outlining main issues
☐ Past agreements—written or verbal
☐ Role of hereditary leaders and Elders
☐ *Indian Act* legislation that pertains to your work

Learn about and stay up-to-date on Indigenous issues

A key to *Working Effectively with Indigenous Peoples*® is to understand their perspectives in advance. Learning a community's history and current issues will enable you to anticipate its priorities and core concerns about your business interests. To do this you can:

- Bookmark our blog *Working Effectively with Indigenous Peoples*® (www.ictinc.ca/blog) which posts new articles weekly on a wide range of topics.
- Sign up for the blog's free newsletter that provides a monthly roundup of articles (www.ictinc.ca/newsletter-sign-up)
- Read the *Report of the Royal Commission on Aboriginal People*
- Read the Truth and Reconciliation Commission's Report and associated 94 Calls-to-Action
- Read books on communities and issues
- Check out the websites of Indigenous organizations
- Subscribe to Indigenous media and newsletters
- Follow Indigenous thought-leaders on social media
- Follow pertinent Indigenous leaders on social media (Facebook and Twitter)

Some Indigenous media sources include:

- **Aboriginal Business Magazine**, (519) 445-0868, ON
- **Alberta Native News**, (780) 421-7966, AB
- **Eagle Feather News**, (866)-323-6397, SK
- **Eastern Door**, (450) 635-3050, QC
- **First Nations Drum**, Vancouver Office (604) 669-5582; Toronto Office (416) 421-4327
- **The First Perspective**, (204) 943-1500, MB
- **Ha-Shilth-Sa**, (250) 724-5757, B.C.
- **Indian Country Today**, Verona, NY
- **Indian Life Magazine**, (204) 661-9333, MB
- **Mi'kmaq—Maliseet Nations News**, (902) 895-6385 NS
- **NunatsiaqOnline**, (867) 979-5357, NU
- **NationTalk**, (416)-987-3126, ON
- **SAY Magazine**, info@saymag.com, MB
- **Wawatay News**, (807) 737-2951, ON
- **Windspeaker**, (780) 455-2700, AB

WORKING EFFECTIVELY TIP:
Be aware of significant events that can compromise your ability to engage people or communities in relationship building.

Google Alerts

Don't forget to take advantage of free services such as Google Alerts. It will let you track any issue, community, or person for free by monitoring the web for specific terms that you want to be alerted on. Pick a term, like xyz First Nation for example and Google will monitor the web for new occurrences of the term. The nice part is that it will send you reports daily, weekly, or monthly based on your specifications. Simply type "Google alerts" into the Google search box for information on how to use the service.

Evaluate

The next step in the **RESPECT** process is to evaluate the information compiled to date—particularly, the potential impact of the community's key issues on your work. What follows is a discussion of issues that can have an impact on operations, and some suggestions for addressing them.

Timing Is Everything

Timing can be everything for the person who is looking to build relationships with a neighbouring Indigenous community. Consider tribes whose cultures revolve around fish and fishing. Those tribes have a very limited window (dictated by nature and regulated by the Department of Fisheries and Oceans) in which to catch enough fish to feed their members through the winter. The priority of fishing can extend to the entire community—including the chief and council. In this environment, it may be next to impossible to get a meeting to happen during the fishing season.

On another note, you may be attempting to talk to a community about scheduling activities, such as pesticide management or tree-thinning. Suppose that you get some resistance and then, with some good questioning, you determine that the community wants to pick berries in your proposed work area at that time of the year. Would you consider changing your plans to make way for their berry-picking? It could mean the difference between deepening resistance and broadening consensus.

Next, consider the issue of death in an Indigenous community. Life is precious in any community, but population is a critical concern to communities struggling to grow as Nations. In this context it is not uncommon for all band operations, including the band office, to shut down completely following the death in a community. Try not to be disappointed if this happens to you.

You Know What They Say About "Assume"

CASE STUDY # 1

Fred was tasked by his organization to consult with First Nations on a particular permit application. He took a look at the map and noticed a reserve in the approximate permit application area. Fred went online and attempted to contact the band to engage them in consultation. After repeated attempts to contact the band he was finally able to reach someone in the band office. He was a little annoyed when he finally got through, and his irritation was apparent in his discussion with the band representative. "I wanted to consult with you. Why didn't you return my call?" The reply was that this was not the traditional territory of the band Fred had contacted and that he needed to contact a different band.

CASE STUDY # 2

George was asked by his organization to deliver a community presentation on an upcoming project. In his research, he identified a band with a hyphenated name, whose band office was located in the area to be traversed by the project. After several meetings with the band, George began to get community consensus on preferred routing and terms of accommodation. Upon review with others in his organization, George learned that there was a problem, and that the consensus may be short-lived. The band council was made up of representatives from the second tribe of the hyphenated name: they had been amalgamated with the tribe of the first name. The project was going to pass through the traditional territory of the first-named tribe of the amalgamated band.

CASE STUDY # 3

Wendy, a new employee with the city, was called into a meeting to discuss a recent incident that some members of the media had branded as racism, and others had dismissed as an unfortunate set of circumstances. The incident was still fresh in the minds of the local Indigenous community and the city wanted to address it.

> **WORKING EFFECTIVELY TIP:** Try to look for the interests and avoid getting locked into positions when working with Indigenous communities.

◇◇◇◇◇◇◇◇◇◇◇◇◇◇◇◇◇◇◇◇◇◇◇◇◇◇◇◇

WORKING EFFECTIVELY TIP:
You may want to call ahead to confirm your scheduled meeting, and if you are traveling a great distance, you may be wise to confirm again while in transit.

◇◇◇◇◇◇◇◇◇◇◇◇◇◇◇◇◇◇◇◇◇◇◇◇◇◇◇◇

Wendy suggested an approach to the local friendship centre. The city moved forward with the idea and Wendy contacted the friendship centre to seek their support for a joint initiative. They agreed to sign an accord at a public event to address the issue and make things better in the future.

On the day of the signing, a local band came forward to protest their exclusion from the accord, noting that one of their members was involved in the original incident. Which group was most affected by the event? If the incident had involved a friendship centre patron, it would have made sense to work with the friendship centre to resolve it. However, this situation should have been resolved with the local band.

Individual Nations and Their Autonomy

CASE STUDY #4

Sandra was asked by her boss to strike a small committee to get input from four Indigenous communities and from local stakeholders on a water treatment issue. She made a list of potential candidates and decided that a particular member from one of those regional communities would be the perfect "representative fit" for this multi-party process.

After several meetings the committee decided on a course of action and made a public announcement to share their findings. Sandra was surprised to receive several awkward phone calls from the other regional communities, expressing serious concern about the findings and course of action. Sandra couldn't figure out what went wrong. See the tip below.

Sacred Lands

Buffalo jumps, sweat lodges, bathing pools, whaling shrines, transformation rocks, first ancestor sites, petroglyphs, spirit dancing, ceremony sites, and birthing spots on the land are just a few examples of sacred sites in Indigenous cultures. If your proposed activity encroaches on such an area, you may encounter fierce resistance from local communities. Your main challenge will be to get them even to talk about such sites. You could experience everything from the cold shoulder to blockades and legal action—depending on the significance of the site, and the degree of trust you have already earned with the community. Some communities will go to the wall to protect their sacred sites. Patience will be required in building the trust needed to get discussion underway.

Strategize

Community Engagement Strategy

With the research and evaluation complete, it's time to put together a strategy for approaching the community that you hope to engage with. You will want to consider individual and organizational approaches to the community's cultural and political issues, planning your verbal and nonverbal communications with care. In this section, we discuss key issues to be addressed in putting together such a strategy.

Strategies for *Working Effectively with Indigenous Peoples®*

Create a formal in-house Indigenous Policy:

- Ensure there is a solid understanding of the need for Indigenous relations;
- Dedicate appropriate staff to form a project team;
- Provide training for project team members;
- Ensure Indigenous awareness training is provided for all staff/managers;
- Ensure staff and financial resources are available to implement the Policy over the long-term;
- Ensure there is support in the upper levels of management;
- Work with local Indigenous leaders and communities to further develop the Policy;
- Incorporate the Indigenous Policy into company/organization's mandate;
- Post the Policy on company/organization's website and other company materials;
- Set and post goals and appoint staff to realize goals;
- Develop an accountability process;
- Develop a system for monitoring progress of goals;
- Communicate the policy to all employees; and
- Communicate progress of policy program throughout organization.

WORKING EFFECTIVELY TIP: Don't assume that a band is necessarily in its own traditional territory. Throughout Canada, bands' reserves were relocated from their traditional territories for different reasons by Indigenous and Northern Affairs Canada.

◇◇◇◇◇◇◇◇◇◇◇◇◇◇◇◇◇◇◇◇◇◇◇◇◇◇◇◇

WORKING EFFECTIVELY TIP:
In a case of band amalgamation,
don't assume that the band chief
and council are able to make
land use decisions regarding
territory that customarily
belongs to someone else.

◇◇◇◇◇◇◇◇◇◇◇◇◇◇◇◇◇◇◇◇◇◇◇◇◇◇◇◇

Create a formal Community Relations Policy:

- Work with the community/ies to establish a community liaison committee;
- Assist community liaison committee with their outreach efforts to contact everyone in the community;
- Appoint staff to work with community liaison committee; and
- Include reports/issues/concerns from community liaison committee into company newsletters.

Community Development Policy:

- Work with communities to identify their community development needs;
- Work with communities to develop an economic development strategy;
- Allocate funding for community infrastructure; and
- Support and attend, if invited, community events.

Cultural Survival

The name of the game for Indigenous Peoples everywhere is cultural survival. Every decision made reflects this value; it's for this reason that decisions can take longer in Indigenous communities. The 7th Generation principle says that all decisions must include consideration of impacts on community members seven generations into the future. This principle is reflected in Indigenous thinking throughout Canada and around the globe.

How might the 7th Generation principle affect your community interaction? First, you have two different perspectives of time. For most companies, the operational time frame is a fiscal year. Things are expected to be done within a fiscal year, or within very few fiscal years. In Indigenous communities, the timeframe is much, much longer.

Second, cultural survival makes Indigenous Peoples do things that do not seem to make sense from a business perspective. For example, suppose that a government or large resource company offers $1 billion to an Indigenous community for their ancestral land. The community refuses outright. The government or resource company is flabbergasted, and states that it is just another example of Indigenous irrationality. But, the decision makes sense in the context of cultural survival. Consider tribes that sold their lands for "beads and bobbles" in centuries gone by.

Those agreements were ill equipped to deal with today's environment and have led to almost insurmountable challenges. Today's tribes will consider cultural survival very seriously when making decisions involving their ancestral land.

Connectivity Principle

The views of many Indigenous Peoples include a principle of connectivity. In this view, everything is connected. The spirit world is connected to the mortal world; the sea is connected to the land; the sky is connected to the ground; and so on.

> **WORKING EFFECTIVELY TIP:**
> There are many dynamics at play when working with Indigenous Peoples and organizations. Try to learn all you can about the identities and allegiances of the participants in a problem before moving to a solution.

On the other hand, it's common for non-Indigenous people to try to isolate the issues in framing their discussions with an Indigenous community. For example, your project will only affect this part of the county, cut block, or valley (Indigenous Peoples will think "territory"). The Indigenous community will likely not consider any issue in isolation. They will think about the cut block, all the other cut blocks in their territory, and the cumulative effects of oil and gas, mining, and logging operations on hunting and fishing throughout the valley before deciding on an issue.

Urban vs. Rural Band

There can be significant issues and differences between a band's reserve residents and its urban members.[2] Some bands work closely with their urban members while others do not. Assess the band's urban/non-urban dynamic to avoid bringing these difficult issues onto the agenda.

Your Timeline is YOUR Problem

Timelines are thorny issues in Indigenous communities. At present, most everyone that goes to a community to do business has a timeline. Do you really want to add yourself to that list? You'll just create resistance and in the end stretch your project's timeline. Also, if you have a tight timeline it can open you up to risks such as judicial reviews, which can add two to five years to your timeline. If you push for the sake of your timeline, you may find that it compromises your current work and future business opportunities in that community. Conversely, you will likely win respect and a more receptive hearing if you approach the community with an attitude marked by interest and willingness to listen, leaving your timeline back in the office.

WORKING EFFECTIVELY TIP:
As a customary rule of protocol, one community cannot speak for another community. Strive to avoid setting up processes, discussions, or consultations where this can become an issue.

Another good way to deal with timeline issues is to have project managers build additional time into business planning processes and policies to accommodate the Indigenous community. Of course, providing capacity funding to the community to be able to work with you can increase your chances of having your requests dealt with in a timely manner.

A Place on the Agenda

Many band chiefs, councils, and administrators don't meet every day; instead they meet periodically and try to cover many agenda items in a single sitting. If you want to make a presentation at the next council meeting, you will want to try to find a good place on the agenda. By a "good place," we mean you don't want to follow a presentation that is likely to be contentious as those emotions will likely spill over onto you and your presentation. A suggestion is to ask for a copy of the agenda in advance of the meeting. If your position on the agenda is unfavourable, then ask for a better position or maybe even be prepared to postpone your presentation until the next council meeting in hopes of a better placement. Also, be aware that with so many items on an agenda, it almost certainly means you won't get all the time you are asking for and you will possibly have to reduce your presentation significantly.

Authority Figures and the Legacy of Residential Schools

A difficult issue that may influence your relationship and work with Indigenous Peoples is that of residential schools and authority figures. Many of the people you will find yourself working with were educated in residential schools—segregated from their families and cultures, possibly subjected to physical and sexual abuse, and almost certainly traumatized by their experiences; many refer to themselves simply as "survivors." They still have many bitter memories associated with those schools and they will tell you that the effects are inter-generational. Be aware that these survivors may have issues with authority figures and that you might just represent authority depending on the role you are playing in communicating with the community.

Men and Women

We have already discussed the rich variety of the traditional social structures of Indigenous Peoples in Canada. In some communities, men occupy centre stage and are the traditional leaders. In other communities, women occupy centre stage and are the traditional leaders. In still other communities, men carry out leadership and administrative roles delegated to them by powerful women who remain in the background.

We have noted the importance of identifying the leadership structures and assessing the governance traditions that apply to the particular community that is of interest to you. Determining the role of gender in decision-making, is a vital part of that assessment. Matching your work team to the community's cultural norms is a good strategy that can help improve working relationships. Conversely, not matching can hinder your progress.

We once had the privilege of learning this lesson first-hand. A colleague had been assigned the "ABC file" with a particular Indigenous community. The community decision-making structure was led by a member of our colleague's opposite gender. By chance, on a later visit to the community we asked the chief, "How is it going with the ABC file?" She replied, "You know how we work here . . . and look who you sent to work with us."

WORKING EFFECTIVELY TIP:
If you encounter resistance such as the cold shoulder, consider asking, "Is there something here that you cannot discuss because it is sacred to the community? If so, I would be happy to agree to not disclose it to the public."

Name Dropping

To name drop or not to name drop, that is the question.

Many people assume that it is okay to name drop as they move from community to community in their work. Communities, like people, have relationships. They can support each other, be in conflict with each other, or be indifferent to each other.

To name drop when the communities are in conflict with each other offers no value and can be outright disastrous. For example, to say "I just came from community X and they really liked what I had to say" may result in the community you are now trying to work with silently saying, "Oh, you're working with them. Hmmm." At which point they are just waiting for you to leave.

On the other hand, to name drop when the communities support each other offers value as you can build on trust between the two communities. For example, "I just came from community X and they really liked what I had to say" may result in the community responding with, "Right on, who did you work with over there?"

Take care to research the type of relationships that exist between communities before name dropping if you are to be effective.

◇◇◇◇◇◇◇◇◇◇◇◇◇◇◇◇◇◇◇◇◇◇◇◇

WORKING EFFECTIVELY TIP:
Be aware that Indigenous Peoples may use the Connectivity Principle when you are speaking with them. Try not to belittle the principle by saying, "We are only here to deal with one issue." Try to accommodate whenever possible.

◇◇◇◇◇◇◇◇◇◇◇◇◇◇◇◇◇◇◇◇◇◇◇◇

People Alignment

The old saying that "You can tell a lot about people by the company they keep" applies to your work in Indigenous communities, whether you realize it or not. For example, if there is an upcoming election and you have aligned yourself with the outgoing chief or council, you may have created a serious people alignment problem for your project. Your selection of consultants to work on your behalf can have similar sensitivity. The reputation of how your hired consultant works with Indigenous Peoples will be considered a reflection on you and your company; hire accordingly.

When attending a multi-party meeting with an Indigenous community, try not to sit close to people whose issues with the community are more contentious than yours as you could inadvertently be perceived as part of that contentious issue.

Also, be wary of the first person who wants to be your friend, and try to get to know those who seem to be avoiding you.

Dress Accordingly

Showing up wearing high heels with lots of makeup and jewellery, or a three piece suit complete with paisley tie and Rockport shoes, for work in an Indigenous community can send the wrong messages. The first message is that you have lots of money to spend. The second message is that you're a "defender of the empire." Both messages can have serious ramifications for your upcoming meeting by setting a tone that may not accurately reflect you or your organization.

Generally speaking, the dress standard in Indigenous communities is quite casual. For both men and women, jeans and casual shirts are usually the norm. Always take your lead from community representatives—if they wear shirts and ties or business suits, then by all means dress accordingly. If your dress code at work requires you to dress in business attire, then try to plan your meetings in a way that allows you to show up at community meetings dressed more casually; at the very least, you can remove the jacket, tie, and jewellery, etc., beforehand. It is also a good idea to wear "weather ready" clothing and footgear.

If you are going to wear Indigenous jewellery, try to choose designs from the community you are working in.

Watch it

I was told this funny story one time by a community leader about a person who really wanted to work with the community. The person spent a long time trying to get a meeting and was finally successful. The meeting was to take place in a remote fly-in community.

The main issue was that the visitor had an annoying habit of checking his watch. He was, of course, worried about the return flight as he did not want to miss it. It got so bad that the community members started to filibuster the follow-up meetings just to see how long they could keep the visitor sitting there.

Gifts

People often ask if they should bring gifts to meetings and other community events. In some cases it may be appropriate and even expected; in others it can actually be offensive—even coming across as bribe. So, how does one know when to bring a gift and what kind of gift is appropriate? The key is simply to ask the host or the administrative person who is helping to set up the meeting on their side, politely, privately, and in advance. Also, be sure to try to evaluate your gift from the perspective of the community.

By the way, if you work for government and you don't have money for gifts, don't bring it up. Also, if you don't have money for gifts, but they are requesting a nominal gift such as tobacco then I would be prepared to pay out of my own pocket for such a gift; it can be really helpful for the relationship building process.

WORKING EFFECTIVELY TIP:

If someone raises residential school issues with you, listen carefully and respectfully. Don't get defensive and don't take it personally—and definitely don't absolve yourself of personal responsibility saying "I wasn't there or I had nothing to do with it." Instead, be prepared to acknowledge it by saying something along the lines of, "thanks for sharing your experiences of residential schools and their impact on you personally, on your family, and on the community. It helps me understand the impact and shows me the importance of the formal apology, baseline compensation, and the Truth and Reconciliation Commission recommendations. I'm hoping that my work with the community will somehow contribute to reconciliation."

Questions they will ask you

Now is also the time to consider the kinds of questions they will ask you: firstly, within the scope of your proposed business venture or project and its potential impacts on the community; secondly, beyond the project to include your personal

WORKING EFFECTIVELY TIP:
Try to match your team's composition with the community's decision-making structure. If women are the decision-makers, then send women. Or, as my mother-in-law would say in that situation, "If you're gonna send a man, at least send a sexy one."

and corporate history and values. Most importantly, we want you to prepare your responses to those anticipated questions in advance of the first meeting. The best source of information for questions they will have is from people who have worked with the community, hopefully recently so you have a good idea of what to expect. I would also ask those same people for advice on how to answer the questions; at the very least, find out what does not work.

Present

If you've worked your way through the RESPECT elements we've covered so far, then the Research, Evaluation, and Strategy elements are in place. Now it's time to begin thinking about your presentation to the Indigenous community. Is the objective of the first meeting just to get acquainted? If you only have money for one meeting, I suggest doing this in hopes of continuing electronically in the future vs. trying to achieve more than one goal at the one meeting. Or is the objective to reach agreement on how to proceed? This next section looks at a range of key presentation issues, including: your first meeting, protocol, mannerisms, and use of colloquialisms.

Your First Meeting

What you might expect depends on many different factors. For example, are you a senior manager or a member of the rank and file? Do you have a large role and lots of responsibility regarding your work? Has your organization's prior relationship with the Indigenous community and its leaders been good, bad, or indifferent? Did your organization insert you at an on-going table because your predecessor was not getting along with the community and/or its leaders?

Try not to arrive too early to your first meeting. If you do, don't sit down beside people you don't know and start conversations about the kids. The last thing you want to do is make friends with someone who is going to get everyone mad at them. When I was doing engagement work, I would hang out by the coffee machine or on the smokers' deck trying to get to know the community people. I don't smoke, but I have found you can get a good conversation going with someone who does.

Another consideration may be to avoid bringing the maps and plans for the project as Indigenous communities will want to get to know who you are as a person before any serious business is conducted. You may have these things with you in a carrying case, but I wouldn't be in a rush to throw them on the table.

Be professional during your first meeting. Follow the lead and mood of those you are meeting with and expect to listen as much as possible. Be prepared to acknowledge should the residential school survivor issues come up.

WORKING EFFECTIVELY TIP:
Avoid annoying habits such as checking your watch; be present in your conversations.

Protocol

It can be customary among First Nations and Indigenous Peoples to acknowledge the host peoples and their territory at the outset of any meeting. The long struggle for respect has been tough, but through it all First Nations and Indigenous Peoples have continued to follow to basic protocols.

It follows, then, that if you want to work effectively with Indigenous Peoples, one of the best ways to do so is to show respect to the people you are working with. This can be established at the beginning of any meeting by following proper protocol and acknowledging the host community, its people, and its territory.

There are two protocol greetings that can be used at the beginning of your meeting. Determining which is appropriate will require some initial research. You will want to know the location of the meeting, and, more specifically, the type of lands you are meeting on (i.e., is your meeting taking place on treaty territory or traditional territory?).

Treaty territory is as it sounds. Lands that have been defined through negotiations and which usually, but not always, have an accompanying map to show you the boundaries. Traditional territory is a little more complicated, but is usually land that has not been defined by treaty but is still used and occupied by Indigenous Peoples. In some cases, you can find maps of traditional territories, but care should be taken in relying solely on a map as the information contained can be subjective.

Once you have tackled the difficult task of determining the type of lands you will be meeting on, you can choose the appropriate greeting. Below you will find two sample acknowledgements for your review, consideration, and adaptation. Keep in mind that these are not the only ways to acknowledge your hosts, and you may learn of alternative greetings more appropriate to your hosts.

◇◇◇◇◇◇◇◇◇◇◇◇◇◇◇◇◇◇◇◇◇◇◇◇

WORKING EFFECTIVELY TIP:
Before name dropping, be sure
to see if they belong to the same
tribal council or treaty council.
Additional research into the
relationships between member
tribal or treaty councils should
show whether there are visible
signs of internal conflict between
individual communities.

◇◇◇◇◇◇◇◇◇◇◇◇◇◇◇◇◇◇◇◇◇◇◇◇

Treaty Territory Protocol
"I would like to thank the _____ for agreeing to meet with us today and for welcoming us to your treaty lands."

Traditional Territory Protocol
"I would like to thank the _____ First Nation(s) for taking the time to meet with us and for inviting us into your traditional territory."

Pronunciations

When it comes to pronunciations people often ask me, "Do I get credit for trying?" No, you get demerits for messing it up. Therefore, be sure to get the pronunciation of the community's name correct. Work with your community contacts or cultural centre representatives to get the pronunciation right. You could also call the band or community office after hours and listen to the recorded voice message several times and practice until you get the pronunciation correct. Check out community websites for clues and be prepared to even seek out and ask for help. If someone from the community is willing to teach you, don't try three times and give up. Keep trying until you get it.

Participating in Cultural Events

At some point during your work with an Indigenous community, you will be expected to participate in a cultural event. It could be an opening prayer, a smudge, or some other form of cultural protocol. It can be very unnerving to participate in a smudge for the first time. When in doubt about what to do, ask the host or a friend of the community to explain the participation process. If all else fails, follow the lead of the people in front of you. Also, sometimes at community events they may want you to try their best food. To say their best food is exotic would be an understatement. To decline such an offering would be a serious faux pas. The best thing you can do is try it with your poker face on and say "Mmm, this is some of the best ooligan oil I have ever tasted."

Eye Contact

Many non-Indigenous people believe that it is important to maintain eye contact during conversation. For many Indigenous Peoples, continuous eye contact may not be expected or even accepted as a courtesy of conversation. We once asked an Elder from a particular Nation for his thoughts on eye contact. This is what he had to say:

> "We never used to have much eye contact. When we did, it was only at the start of the meeting. After that, it was not considered important to maintain eye contact."

For residential school survivors, eye contact with school or church officials often led to physical punishment.

When you have the opportunity to attend an Indigenous community event, look at people's eyes and where they are gazing—their gaze is usually not on the speaker. This is not a sign of disrespect. An Indigenous listener is usually more interested in following the speaker's words than where s/he is gazing.

I also had another elder say this:

> "If I had not seen you for a long time, maybe four months or more, then I would look you briefly in the eye and that would be it. Then I would go back to looking around because if we were looking at each other in the eye, we could miss supper going by."

Handshakes and Indigenous Peoples

When it comes to a handshake and Indigenous Peoples, what could possibly go wrong?

Offering a hand for a handshake is a fairly common social practice when meeting people. This works most of the time, but we do have to remember that when we are working with Indigenous Peoples we are working across cultures with individuals in their own right and that some Indigenous People do not shake hands therefore are not expecting, or are comfortable with, a handshake. With this in mind, we have to understand and be prepared to offer a hand and not have one offered in return.

Should this happen to you, then be sure not to read anything into the fact that someone from the community didn't offer to shake hands with you when you

WORKING EFFECTIVELY TIPS:

1. Be sure to ask the person with whom you are setting up the meeting to help you with proper greeting and meeting protocol before you arrive.

2. Keep in mind that your spirit and sincerity can matter more than your particular words.

offered a hand first. Do not interpret it as a sign of disrespect, or a sign that they don't like you, when it could possibly be a sign that they simply don't shake hands.

So what do you do if you offer a handshake and none comes back? Be prepared to be left hanging! To save yourself from this uncomfortable situation, pretend to scratch your shoulder in a looked-like-a-handshake-but-then-turned-into-a-shoulder-scratch manoeuvre.

Another handshake scenario is when you offer a handshake and they offer you the left hand instead—there is no shaking or squeezing and it can go on for an uncomfortably long period. Remember, they are just being polite and your job is to roll with the punches.

Two last thoughts on the handshake:

1. When in the north working with the Inuit, or all northerners for that matter, be sure to take your glove off when shaking hands.
2. And lastly, you know you are doing really well when you are given a hug and not a handshake!

Acronyms

We have attended many meetings in Indigenous communities and have witnessed first hand the overuse of acronyms by other visitors—which may make great sense, but only to those using them. Remember where you are and who your audience is. Not only will many in your Indigenous audience be unfamiliar with your acronyms, they might not even want to learn them!

Technical Terms

Indigenous Peoples are like audiences anywhere in the sense that they want a presentation that they can relate to and understand. One comment we often hear Indigenous community members say is, "How come the presenters have to use such big words?"

Make your presentation appeal to your audience. If the audience is strictly technical people, then technical terms or jargon are welcome. Otherwise, use language that the layperson will understand. If in doubt, explain things in plain language that everyone can understand. I usually tell my clients to use written and verbal communications at about a grade eight level. This helps communicate with a large audience.

Colloquialisms

When trying to work effectively with Indigenous People, it is wise to avoid the use of colloquialisms. Many colloquial expressions used in popular communication carry connotations that may offend at least some of the people you will meet.

Here are some expressions you should take pains to avoid:

Circle the wagons

Circle the wagons translates to the savages are coming. We learned in an earlier chapter that not all relationships with Indigenous Peoples required a circling of the wagons.

Low man on the Totem Pole

Totem poles are very sacred items to the people who carve and display them. In some Indigenous communities, being low on the totem pole is actually a higher honour than being on the top.

Too many chiefs and not enough Indians

A very good friend helped us with this colloquialism. He tells a story about a meeting he attended in the course of his consulting work with a large organization. The organization had many people from many different departments working on a relationship-building initiative. During the meeting it became evident that direction was lacking. Our friend then said, "We have a problem. It seems to me that we have too many chiefs and not enough Indians."

He said it was perhaps the most embarrassing moment of his life; the silence that ensued went on forever. Fortunately, he had a good relationship in the community and that moment became a long-running joke around the multi-party table, with the Indigenous representatives taking every opportunity to remind him of the "Indian chief surplus problem." Needless to say, such expressions no longer have a place in his business vocabulary.

Indian summer

The inference is that all Indians are late and that an Indian Summer is a late summer. Many people in response have said, "But I use this phrase in the highest

WORKING EFFECTIVELY TIP:
Let others lead the handshake. If they grab your hand firmly and squeeze really hard twice while doing the salt and pepper shaker action, then do all that in return.

You don't lead in case they don't do any of that. There have been situations in which Indigenous people have been caught off guard in a handshake situation and have had their hands squeezed too hard and have been injured. Not a good way to kick off your Indigenous relations.

respect as a beautiful time of year." Remember it may not be your intention to offend anyone, but the phrase has a history and, by using this term, you may have a negative impact on the people that you are trying to work with.

Indian time

Again, the inference is that all Indians are late. Keep in mind that you may hear this being used by Indigenous Peoples, but don't let this use lull you into thinking it is okay to use this term. This is an example of stereotyping and the use of stereotypes between members of the same group is different than the use of stereotypes between members of different groups, whatever the group's dynamics (i.e., race, culture, nation, sport, or gender).

Pow wow

"We need to get together and have a pow wow to discuss this." A pow wow can be a significant community event and the everyday reference to it may annoy some members of the community.

Many moons ago

As in, "That was something we did many moons ago."

Off the reservation

I have two issues with this. The first is that it is an American term and if you use it in Canada they will know you are a rookie and treat you accordingly. It also is commonly used to make people sound crazy. I'm sure that it is not the best way to communicate.

Keep in mind you don't actually have to do what I'm telling you to do. These are just the "suffering is optional" recommendations. If you do choose any of these colloquialisms or forget not to use them, then you face at least an extra hour of meeting time if not more.

Terms to Avoid

Stakeholder is a commonly used business term that should be avoided at all costs when working with Indigenous Peoples. If the "Rod and Gun Club" (a stakeholder) doesn't like what you are doing, they can lobby their MP or MLA to try to effect changes. If an Indigenous community doesn't like what you are doing, they have the ability to launch legal action that puts your project in immediate jeopardy. In this context, Indigenous Peoples are not stakeholders because they have constitutionally protected rights and are used to dealing with Canada, provinces, and territories on a Nation-to-Nation basis. We suggest you use *rights holder* as an alternative choice. Also, you could try breaking out Indigenous Peoples by saying something along the lines of "we are here as we are talking to federal, provincial, Indigenous, and local government as well as other stakeholders."

Equality is another term that should be avoided when working with Aboriginal Peoples. When Aboriginal Peoples hear the term equality or equal they hear that they have to give up their constitutionally protected rights or they hear we can be equal only if they give up their human rights to be who they are as a people.

Pre-history implies the history of Indigenous Peoples began with the arrival of Europeans. In reality, each individual Indigenous culture has its own creation story that certainly pre-dates the arrival of Europeans in what is now known as Canada. A better way to divide the timeline is pre- and post-contact.

A related caution is to avoid the concept that the Americas were *discovered* (which we covered earlier in Part I), but just to refresh your memory: when Christopher Columbus *arrived* in the Americas, there were an estimated 100 million Indigenous Peoples living there at the time.

Canada's Indigenous Peoples implies ownership. Canada doesn't own Indigenous Peoples. Avoid the possessive "our" when referring to Indigenous Peoples in Canada. They are not "our" Indigenous Peoples and they are not "Canada's Indigenous Peoples." Try using *Indigenous Peoples in Canada* or *First Peoples in Canada*.

Crown Lands could land you in a bench-clearing brawl at your meeting. Instead use *treaty* or *traditional territory*.

What you people should do is what Indian Affairs has been saying for over 140 years and all of the "help" they have delivered hasn't really helped them.

Oral Societies

Most of the pre-contact Indigenous People of the Americas lived in oral societies. Very few of them had written languages or histories, but that is not to say that they didn't record their histories in other ways. One of the most important ways was through the oral tradition of storytelling. The Supreme Court of Canada has declared that oral histories must be given the same legal weight as written histories in Aboriginal rights and title cases.[3]

In Indigenous culture, your word is more important than anything written on a piece of paper. At all costs, you must make sure that you protect your word and integrity in all your dealings on behalf your organization. Nothing can damage

◇◇◇◇◇◇◇◇◇◇◇◇◇◇◇◇◇◇◇◇◇◇◇◇◇◇◇◇

WORKING EFFECTIVELY TIP:
In an oral society, the spoken word can be more important than any written contract. Guard your word from changes in organizational direction. Don't offer things that you're not certain you can deliver and definitely follow-up on the things you said you would deliver.

◇◇◇◇◇◇◇◇◇◇◇◇◇◇◇◇◇◇◇◇◇◇◇◇◇◇◇◇◇◇

your reputation more than having to say, "Things have changed and I will no longer be able to deliver what I promised."

Because the traditional mode of Indigenous communication is oral, speech nuances like tone, tempo, volume, and inflections can be very important. Be aware and try to match the community style of speech if you can without trying to copy their accent. Also, don't be in a rush to respond until you figure out the tempo, etc.

Have they really finished speaking?

A First Nation chief was making introductory comments to a meeting of company and government employees. The talk went on for a few minutes; then the chief paused to gather more thoughts. The lead person for the company thought that the chief had finished and began to respond to his comments. The company spokesman completed a sentence or two before the chief interrupted him by saying, "I'm not finished yet."

Sense of Humour

Do you have a good sense of humour? Can you laugh at yourself? Can you take it when people are laughing at you? We have seen many visitors welcomed to Indigenous community meetings with humour that sometimes bites a little. Go with the flow. Being teased with humour can actually be a sign of acceptance—signalling that they may want to work with you and are trying to get you to conform to group norms.

Where Are You From?

One of the better questions to ask when getting to know an Indigenous person is "Where are you from?" It's more a question of who are your people and where is your territory. This is different from "Where do you live?" If the person replies "I'm living in Vancouver" you may have uncovered an important clue about the role that person plays in the community. It could be that this person has left the community temporarily for education or management training, and is being groomed as a future leader. Or, it could be that he or she was adopted out and does not have intimate community knowledge or involvement. If the reply describes a place in the First Nation's traditional territory, then you might guess that the person is more connected to the community, and therefore is more knowledgeable and supportive regarding its interests. In any case, more questions are probably needed before you can properly assess this person's place in, and perspective on, the community.

The Concept of Family

The concept of family means different things to different people within Indigenous communities. You might be tempted to assume that "family" means immediate family, including husband or wife, children, and perhaps grandparents. For some Indigenous communities, the concept of family can have broader meaning. For example, first cousins can be considered as close as brothers and sisters. This concept can mean a larger role for families and more family members in community activities. In a few cases, I have seen the concept of family applied to the whole community—meaning that the whole community, all 377 people, are a family grouping.

Communal Thinking

CASE STUDY #5

> John worked for a government agency that was actively involved in granting a permit to a resource company. It was his responsibility to consult with the band to minimize infringement of its constitutionally protected rights, and to negotiate appropriate accommodation regarding any such infringement.
>
> After several meetings, John ascertained that the company's planned activities would constitute minimal infringement of the community's Aboriginal rights, and that the community would accept the proposed benefits as fair accommodation. Based on this, John decided to recommend that a permit be issued, despite concerns from the band chief that he needed more time for community discussion. The issue had been put before the people, but a small number of members still had concerns. John's main motivation was his manager's timeline for completing the job. The permit was issued and months later the resource company had a road block on an important access road.

WORKING EFFECTIVELY TIP: Non-Indigenous conversations often follow a brisk pattern of "point-counterpoint." When working with Indigenous Peoples, be sure to leave time for the speaker to finish, especially in a new relationship.

What went wrong?

Read recent court decisions on Aboriginal rights and title and you will find that they reference communally held rights. Generally speaking, Aboriginal rights are collectively held on behalf of the entire community. Therefore, any decision regarding the use of those lands is a potential infringement of the rights of the whole community.

The key issue in the case study was the timeline. The community plans on being in the area forever. They feel no pressure to make short-term decisions on matters that can affect the long-term interests of the community and its future generations. The larger the decision, the more the community will be involved.

It is also important to note that usually such sensitive decisions are not made under leadership discretion or by majority rule, but rather by broad community support. What can you do to avoid getting into trouble? Allow more time in your project timeline to accommodate a broader community decision-making process and accede to a chief's request for more time for additional community discussions.

Evaluate

Any meeting with an Indigenous community, or one of its members, should be followed by an evaluation. The process is fairly simple.

Ask yourself:

- How did the meeting go?
- What questions did the community members ask?
- What questions remain outstanding?
- What concerns did the community raise about your proposed project?
- How satisfied were they with your answers?
- What community concerns about the project remain outstanding?
- How critical are those concerns to the viability of the project?
- What was the tone of the meeting?
- What was the apparent perspective of the chief and council members?
- What was the apparent perspective of community Elders?
- Who holds effective political power in the community?
- What do those power brokers think about your project?
- Conduct a risk assessment again to verify your research.

Indigenous Community Communications

Indigenous communities communicate internally in various ways. Sometimes there is efficient communication and other times there is not. Because Aboriginal rights are collectively held, it's important to know if the community is aware of what is going on. Here are some things you should know about the process of Indigenous community communication.

- As we've discussed, Indigenous Peoples are traditionally oral societies. Within the framework of an oral society, word can travel remarkably quickly from one person to the next. This can occur in community events, on the telephone, through social media, or in casual conversation. The combination of better telecommunications' infrastructure in many remote communities, combined with the rise of social media, has also had an impact on community communications. Facebook seems to be coming out as the leader of the platforms adopted in communities.

- Community communications may not be structured the way that a corporate person would expect. If you were to call the band office and ask to speak to the Communications Manager, chances are you would find there is no such person. Many communities do not have a formal structured communications process with a Vice President or Director of Communications. Work will have to be done to figure out the informal communications process and structure. Key questions to ask yourself include:
  - Do chief, council, and band administration communicate regularly and well with the community?
  - Is community communication fast or slow? If there is no formal structure, then assume that communication is slow until you determine otherwise.

- Lack of communication, poor communication, or slow communication. If you think communications are going to be an issue, then be prepared to suggest or offer help to ensure that key issues are being communicated.

- Single family dwellings with multiple families. Overcrowded housing is an issue on reserves Canada-wide. Direct mail campaigns can be problematic if this issue is not taken into account as not all residents of a dwelling will have access to the mail.

For big decisions, the more the community knows, and the wider the sharing of that community knowledge, the better the decision and the stronger the support.

Customize

A great deal of work will have been completed upon reaching this level of working effectively with Indigenous communities. Now is the time to customize your work: incorporating the feedback received and requests made during your journey through the **RESPECT** process.

When designing your work process or plan, consider customization of the following areas according to the needs and priorities of the Indigenous community with whom you are working:

- Legal capacity
- Human resources capacity
- Communications capacity
- Financial capacity
- Timelines
- Workforce development capacity
- Business development capacity

Of particular importance in this Customize step is "community communication." You need to find out if the full community is receiving your information or message. If not, then you must find a way to reach the full community. Consider the following methods:

- Organize presentations in town hall format
- Advertise in community and regional newspapers
- Conduct a direct mail campaign to individual community members
- Make presentations on community radio or television
- Distribute joint newsletters with the community
- Post information on community bulletin boards at the band office, recreation centre, health centre etc. if so permitted

The preceding list is not exhaustive. Two key points here are:

1. you must ensure that the whole community knows what is happening **from your organization's perspective;** and
2. you must ensure that you are receiving widespread community feedback and input **from the community perspective.**

When you have concluded the Customize step, the next move is to go back to the community with another presentation—thereby demonstrating your commitment to adapt your plans to accommodate the community's key needs and concerns—and seek the community's further feedback.

Transform

If you and your organization have truly followed this **RESPECT** process, you are now ready to transform your Indigenous community relationship. Return to the community to present your Customized presentation. The ideal presentation should include a synopsis of the initial presentation, identification of issues and concerns, and steps taken or are in-progress to address issues and concerns.

Transformation is an ongoing process. It will take continued commitment to transform an arm's length (and possibly adversarial) relationship to a mutually beneficial long-term relationship and we believe it can be done. Keep in mind that on a personal level, you should strive to maintain the community relationships that you have developed by working through the **RESPECT** process—for the long-term.

Specific things to do to support the transformation process include but are not limited to:

- Continuing to participate in community cultural events;
- Sending information on project employment and procurement opportunities, and on related training and scholarship opportunities;
- Sending information on corporate donations, or other programs, that may be of interest to the community;
- Continuing to stay up-to-date on the community and its issues through media clipping services; and
- Visiting the community when you don't need or want something.

Again, your intention must be to sustain long-term and mutually beneficial relationships between your organization and the Indigenous community. Nothing can hurt you like calling only when you need something. We believe that you can do more on an informal basis than you can in numerous formal meetings. **At all times, remember that you and your organization are in many cases doing business with a culture, not with another business.**

Do and Don't—A Check List

The following are some things to do and not to do when working with Indigenous Peoples:

DO:

- Research the community and governing parties before going to the community.
- Plan activities by taking into account the timing of issues such as fishing, berry picking, or a death in a community, and take appropriate actions.
- Take training on "Working Effectively with Indigenous Peoples®" before you start.
- Thank the community for the invitation into their traditional territory. For example, "I would like to thank the _____ First Nation(s) for agreeing to meet with us and inviting us into your traditional territory."
- Use caution when shaking hands. The typical North American elbow grab and double pump may not be needed or appreciated.
- Try to establish a relationship and meet before you need something.
- Recognize that there are many dynamics at play when working with Indigenous Peoples and organizations; try to learn about those dynamics in advance.
- Try to match your team's composition with the community's decision-making structure.
- Recognize that individual communities like their autonomy (one Indigenous community cannot speak for another); avoid setting up processes, discussions, or consultations where this could be an issue.
- Do everything you can to avoid sacred land issues by asking good questions and gaining understanding.
- Learn about and stay up-to-date on Indigenous issues and perspectives.
- Understand that internal community communications happen in many different ways and can impact your organization's ability to work effectively with those communities.
- Consider dressing casually for work in the community. In many cases, band offices have more casual dress policies than does corporate Canada.
- Be prepared to have your meetings recorded via microphone or video camera as some communities have had problems in their dealings with people who were less than honourable in remembering what they said.
- Approach issues with a joint problem-solving attitude.
- Know the difference between a band chief and a hereditary chief before you visit an Indigenous community.

- Be prepared to possibly meet both band chiefs and hereditary chiefs on the same day and in the same meeting.
- Honour all your agreements, especially your oral agreements. Traditionally, Indigenous communities are oral societies and oral agreements are even more important than written agreements.
- Be aware of who you are perceived to be aligned with when working in the community and manage those "people alignment" dynamics.
- Be aware that Aboriginal rights are communally held and that the whole community may need to be involved in the decision-making process.
- Be aware that cultural survival is a fundamental driver of an Indigenous community's decision-making process.
- Expect to participate in cultural events and ask for protocol guidance from the host.
- Ask people "where they are from" to learn about where they likely stand on community issues.
- Seek strategic placement for your organization's issues on community meeting agendas.
- Ask the Indigenous community how they want to be consulted. What are their expectations?
- Be prepared to say that you are having a problem and that you are seeking their thoughts on how to solve it.
- Anticipate questions they may have of your organization and prepare answers to those questions.

DON'T:
- Use acronyms in your communications with Indigenous Peoples.
- Use colloquialisms in your communications with Indigenous Peoples.
- Tell the community you are there to speak to its members as stakeholders.
- Tell them that you have a timeline and that they have to meet it.
- Tell them that you have to treat them equally with others.
- Tell them what dates to meet; instead, ask which dates would work best for their community.
- Go to them with a completed draft plan for your project before consultation has started.
- Expect to consult with the same community in the same way on different issues.
- Expect to consult with different communities in the same way on similar issues.
- Assume a band is necessarily in its own territory.

- Assume that the band chief and council are able to make land use decisions regarding other Peoples territories.
- Confuse potluck with potlatch.
- Confuse reservations with reserves.
- Refer to them as Indians or Natives; instead use Indigenous Peoples, First Nations, Métis Peoples, or Inuit.
- Say that some of my best friends are: Indigenous Peoples, Indian, First Nation, Métis Peoples, or Inuit.
- Ask them if they know well-known First Nations personalities—for example, Adam Beach or Thomas King.
- Tell them that you prefer a municipal style of government to a traditional government.
- Tell them that we should all be equal.
- Ask them if they are going to be Canadian when this is all over.
- Impose or expect direct eye contact.
- Feel that you must answer or fill the silent periods during discussions. These silent periods can be longer than you are accustomed to, and may be needed for thought formulation. Try to ensure that the speaker has finished before you contribute to the conversation.

So there you have it. We have tried to provide the benefit of many years of training and experience into the contents of this book in the hopes that people will be able to work more effectively with Indigenous Peoples. We wish you much luck in your endeavours and would welcome feedback on the book should you wish to share. Please feel free to share by emailing info@ictinc.ca, and good luck working with the communities.

D. SCENARIOS—
TEST YOUR KNOWLEDGE

THIS SECTION OF the book covers some common scenarios to test your knowledge on some of the ideas presented thus far. The numbered scenarios are in no particular order and are based on very common issues. Each scenario includes three choices or responses. Your task is simple: read the scenario, make a choice, and then turn to the page as directed to see result of your choice.

Scenario 1—Is it best to approach chief and council?
The boss has finally agreed to start working with local Indigenous communities and more specifically local First Nations. You get called into the office to discuss the approach. The boss suggests that the best place to start is with chief and council and urges you to send a letter of introduction requesting a meeting.

What action would you take?

A. I agree with my boss and send a letter of introduction requesting a meeting. (Answer on page 161)
B. I need more information. (Answer on page 161)
C. I suggest a different approach. (Answer on page 161)

Scenario 2—What's the best term?
Your boss calls you into the office looking for your advice on how to respond to a

local Indigenous community about a request for something... for example, a set aside of jobs or corporate donations. Your boss explains that the request is sensitive because they are looking for something very specific that would not be available to everyone. The boss is insistent that the following letter/message be delivered by you in person at the community office.

Dear xyz Community:

We are in receipt of your request and would like you know that we are unable to comply with this request as such a request would not treat all applicants "equally." We have a firm belief that every community should be treated equally and fairly and our fulfillment of such a request would violate our belief. We look forward to your continued support of our business and activities.

Sincerely,
Mr. I.M. Wright

What Action would you take?
A. I agree with my boss and deliver the message in person? (Answer on page 162)
B. I need more background information. (Answer on page 162)
C. I will suggest small changes in wording and will deliver the message in person. (Answer on page 162)

Scenario 3—What's the best term to use at a speaking engagement?
The boss calls you into the office to help with a speech to be delivered in downtown metropolis next week. The topics to be covered are corporate initiatives underway with local communities. It's to be delivered to a diverse audience of people including, non-Indigenous people, Inuit, First Nation, and Métis Peoples. You learn the boss intends to use the term "native" and "non-native" in the speech and wants you to confirm that it is ok.

A. I see no concerns with the terminology and wish the boss good luck with the speech. (Answer on page 163)
B. I have concerns and suggest appropriate terminology. (Answer on page 163)
C. I need more background information. (Answer on page 164)

Scenario 4—Should you get all the different communities to meet in the same place?

The boss has finally decided to start the big Indigenous initiative. You are called into the office to give input as to the best approach for meeting all of the communities given the time and the budget constraints imposed by the executive. The initial thoughts presented are to have one big meeting in a central location and invite a whole bunch of communities from around the province to attend and provide input. The boss hands over the file to you and says get to work.

What action would you take?

A. I agree with my boss and start organizing the central meeting. (Answer on page 164)
B. I need more information. (Answer on page 164)
C. I suggest a different approach. (Answer on page 164)

Indigenous Understanding—A Quiz

The following multiple choice questions are intended to test your knowledge of terms relating to Indigenous People. Circle the correct answer.

Indigenous Peoples are:
A. All Indigenous people of Canada
B. Indians (Status and non-Status) and Métis
C. Defined in the Constitution
D. All of the above

Status Indian is:
A. A person defined as an Indian under the *Indian Act*
B. An Indigenous person of high rank
C. A person of Métis ancestry
D. None of the above

Non-status Indian is:
A. A person who claims Indigenous ancestry
B. A person who doesn't meet the criteria for registration as a Status Indian
C. A person who has chosen not to be registered under the *Indian Act*
D. All of the above

Band is:

A. A musical group; i.e. Red Bone
B. A body of Indians
C. Defined in the *Indian Act*
D. B and C only

First Nation:

A. Is an Indigenous governing body organized by a community
B. Can include Status and non-Status Indians
C. Can be one band or include several different bands
D. Can replace the term band
E. All of the above

Métis is:

A. A person who self-identifies as a member of a Métis community
B. Any person with mixed Indian and European heritage
C. A person who has some proof of an ancestral connection to the historic Métis community whose collective rights they are exercising
D. A person who holds proof of acceptance by the modern Métis community
E. Only A, C, and D

Reserve is:

A. Defined under section 2 of the Indian Act
B. Land set apart by the federal government for the use and benefit of a band
C. Title to land vested in the Crown
D. All of the above

Treaty is:

A. A petition to the United Nations
B. An opening offer in the negotiation process
C. A "sweetener" offer added late in the negotiation process
D. A formal agreement between governments, or between the Crown and an Indigenous People or Peoples
E. None of the above

Answers can be found on page 165

Answers to Scenarios

Scenario 1

A. Weeks go by with no response and you are left trying to understand why and what to do next. The chances of success using this approach are definitely hit and miss. This approach may work in some circumstances but can often not be the best approach. A better approach would be to use the first three letters of the **RESPECT** concept to arrive at your strategy. Do the Research, Evaluation, and formulate the Strategy about where to start before beginning and new relationship.

B. The R, E, and S in the **RESPECT** concept represent the steps that should be taken when starting out to work with Indigenous Peoples. **Research; Evaluate; Strategize**. You should formulate a strategy based on the evaluation of your research. For example, if you are a retailer selling pharmaceuticals you may find in your research that the Indigenous community's Health Department handles all issues in relation to health. In this situation the best place to start would not be chief and council but with the Health Department of the Indigenous community. Another example would be if you are doing consultation for the government or a developer; to start with the Rights and Title office, Lands Department, Natural Resources Coordinator, or possibly even the Economic Development officer of the community with whom you are seeking to work.

C. In this scenario much time could be saved by doing **Research** and **Evaluation** before suggesting a **Strategy** as suggested in the **RESPECT** concept. Your suggestion would be to do this before coming up with a strategy. Formulate a strategy based on the evaluation of your research. For example, if you are a retailer selling pharmaceuticals you may find in your research that the Health Department handles all issues in relation to health. In this situation the best place to start would not be chief and council but with the Health Department of the Indigenous community. Another example would be if you are doing consultation for the government or a developer, start with the Rights and Title office, Lands Department, Natural Resources Coordinator, or possibly even the Economic Development officer of the community with whom you are seeking to work.

Scenario 2

A.   You better call for help. You head out and deliver you message in person to the XYZ community. To your surprise the response is negative and angry. No sooner did the community members finish reading the message did the verbal feedback start and continue for a prolonged period of time. When it ended so did the meeting. By the time you got to the office your boss had heard about the incident from the community leader who informed your boss that neither you nor the boss are welcome back and to not attempt to contact them again.

B.   YAY! You did it. Congratulations. You change the equality wording to something else and get a much better reception from the community. You agree to at least look internally at what you can do and offer to get back to the community as soon as is possible. The main message is to avoid using the terms like equality as the word can be interpreted differently and be offensive to some Indigenous Peoples.

C.   The equality principle is important to many people and organizations in Canada. One big challenge or issue with the equality principle is trying to define what it means. Some people think it means one person one vote. From the perspective of voting, if 10 people don't want development and 11 people do, are the 10 that don't being treated equally when the development goes ahead? Other people think it means equality in law. From the perspective of the law, why can one local government pass laws allowing the building of a 20 storey building while another local government can pass laws making it illegal to build a building over five stories? Is that equal?

Equality from the perspective of Indigenous Peoples has a different meaning. To Aboriginal Peoples constitutionally protected section 35 rights represent the legal and inherent "right to be who we are" within confederation. Unlike other cultures who came here at a later date for whatever reason, Indigenous Peoples did not come here from anywhere. They have to figure out how to be Indigenous Peoples here in Canada because there is no other place on earth for that to happen. From this perspective Aboriginal rights are both legal rights, but more importantly, human rights and not race-based rights, un-equal rights, or special rights as they are often characterized.

It follows, then, that calls for "equal" rights are seen as a direct threat to the legal and human rights of Aboriginal Peoples and Nations within Canada because it would mean giving up who you are to be like everyone else. This differs from other Canadians who have immigrated to Canada now or in the past. For example, consider an Italian person's perspective who, in coming to Canada from Italy, knows that living in Canada has its benefits and obligations. That same Italian person, though, worries less about the Italian culture, language, land base, religion, and political system as that cultural group, language, and land base will continue to thrive in Italy.

In this scenario, Mr. Wright is going to tell the Indigenous community that he has to treat the community "equally" to everyone else. The negative feedback you will likely receive will be triggered by his use of the term equally. In some cases, the negative feedback is being provided to try and help people like Mr. Wright to understand the issues. In other cases, the community or individuals will be sufficiently offended that Mr. Wright's organization and Mr. Wright will never be welcome in the XYZ community. In still other cases, the potential response would be for the community to sit back quietly and then wait for you to leave and never invite you back.

WORKING EFFECTIVELY WITH INDIGENOUS PEOPLES® TIP: Do use terminology or expressions that convey the message but do not include negative buzz words like "equality" or "equally" in your discussions and correspondence with Indigenous Peoples. Also, for some organizations it may be mutually beneficial to use resources, inputs and outputs strategically as set asides so plan ahead and include them to your competitive advantage. Specific offerings could include jobs or business development or even offering to jointly select the firm to doing the archaeological overview.

Scenario 3

A. The response to the speech from the audience the following week was less than favourable. One participant stands up in front of the whole group and states that they are not native and therefore not restless (a reference to the colloquialism "the natives are restless"). They further state that no one should do business with people who do not even know what to call the people they are dealing with. The boss informs you of the outcome and you know there has been a loss of confidence.

B. You suggest the use of the terms "non-Indigenous people" and "Indigenous Peoples." This is an excellent move. While it is possible to slide by with the "native" terminology, someone will eventually split hairs on it and it does not help to build long term relationships.

C. The use of the term "native" has the potential to be problematic. For start-ers, people like to be called who they are and not always something out of an old Hollywood movie. It should also be pointed out that some organizations and Indigenous Peoples still call themselves native. So what is a working effec-tively practitioner to do? The best advice is to always mirror how people refer to themselves. If the delivery of a speech is to a diverse audience then start with Indigenous Peoples and acknowledge all of the different groups.

> For example, "*We are committed to working with Indigenous Peoples and would like to acknowledge First Nations, Métis, and Inuit peoples in the audience.*"
>
> Another example might be "*I would like to acknowledge the Indigenous Peo-ples that we are working with, including the XYZ Indian Band and the ABC First Nation.*" If delivery of the speech was within a First Nations community then it would be appropriate to say we are committed to working with the ABC First Nation.

Scenario 4

A. This approach has proven to be disastrous on many different occasions. This is one of them. The central meeting being contemplated will bring together a number of diverse groups with different, competing, and opposing interests to the table. These types of meetings tend to go sideways and you are now two steps back instead of moving forward.

B. It is not always risky but can be risky to bring together diverse groups. What always gets people in trouble though is when people do things because it will be easy and quick. Sometimes things that look easy and quick can be the opposite as in the case of bringing together diverse groups with different, competing, and opposing interests. Bringing people to such an environment can create a situation for conflict not just with the organizer but the other participants. If conflict does occur it takes away the opportunity to move forward as planned and the meeting will suffer. Some detailed research would help here to find out which communities

C. Congratulations! This a good move, especially if your suggestion includes doing research on the communities to determine which ones will work together well and which ones will not.

Answers to Quiz

Indigenous Peoples are:
All indigenous people of Canada. This includes Indians (Status and non-Status), Métis, and Inuit people (as defined in the *Constitution Act, 1982*).

Status Indian is:
A person defined as an Indian under the *Indian Act*. Also may be referred to as a registered Indian.

Non-Status Indian is:
D. All of the above. A Non-status Indian is a person who claims Indigenous ancestry, but does not meet the criteria for registration or has chosen not to be registered under the *Indian Act*.

Band is:
D. B and C only. A band is an organizational structure which represents a particular body of Indians as defined under the *Indian Act*.

First Nation(s):
E. All of the above. The term First Nation has no generally agreed on definition. It can refer to a single individual; single band; many bands; an Indigenous governing body, organized and established by an Indigenous community; or the Indigenous community itself.

Métis is:
Only A, C, and D. A Métis person is a person who self-identifies as a member of a Métis community; has some proof of an ancestral connection to the historic Métis community whose collective rights they are exercising; and holds proof of acceptance by the modern Métis community.

Reserve is:
D. All of the above. Reserve is defined in section 2 of the *Indian Act* as a tract of land that has been set apart by the federal government for the use and benefit of an Indian band. The legal title to reserve land is vested in the federal government.

Treaty is:
D. A formal agreement between governments or between the Crown and an Indigenous People or Peoples.

GLOSSARY

Aboriginal Consultation
The Crown has a legal duty to engage in meaningful consultation whenever it has reason to believe that its policies or actions, directly or indirectly, might infringe upon actual or claimed Aboriginal interests, rights or title. As the Supreme Court of Canada said in 2004:

> "The nature and scope of the duty of consultation will vary with the circumstances... At all stages, good faith on both sides is required. The common thread on the Crown's part must be 'the intention of substantially addressing [Aboriginal] concerns' as they are raised through a meaningful process of consultation... Meaningful consultation may oblige the Crown to make changes to its proposed action based on information obtained through consultations...The fact that third parties [industry] are under no duty to consult or accommodate Aboriginal concerns does not mean that they can never be liable to Aboriginal Peoples. If they act negligently in circumstances where they owe Aboriginal Peoples a duty of care, or if they breach contracts with Aboriginal Peoples or deal with them dishonestly, they may be held legally liable. But they cannot be held liable for failing to discharge the Crown's duty to consult."[1]

Aboriginal Interest
A broad term referring to the range of rights and entitlements that may arise from long use and occupation of traditional territories by Aboriginal people. Application

of common law, statute law, treaty provisions, and the constitutional protection provided to "... the existing aboriginal and treaty rights of the Aboriginal people of Canada" by section 35 of *The Constitution Act, 1982*, to the facts of the particular case, determines the scope of "Aboriginal interest."

Aboriginal Peoples

Defined in the *Constitution Act, 1982* to include all Aboriginal people of Canada—Status Indians, non-Status Indians, Métis, and Inuit people.

Aboriginal Rights

- practices, traditions, or customs which are integral to the distinctive culture of an Aboriginal society and were practiced prior to European contact, meaning they were rooted in the pre-contact society;
- must be practiced for a substantial period of time to have formed an integral part of the particular Aboriginal society's culture;
- must be an activity that is a central, defining feature which is independently significant to the Aboriginal society;
- must be distinctive, meaning it must be distinguishing and characteristic of that culture;
- must be given priority over all other land uses, after conservation measures;
- must meet a continuity requirement, meaning that the Aboriginal society must demonstrate that the connection with the land in its customs and laws has continued to the present day;
- may be the exercise in a modern form of an activity that existed prior to European contact;
- may be regulated by government, but only by legislation explicitly directed at a compelling and substantial objective such as the conservation and management of natural resources;
- do not include an activity that solely exists because of the influence of European contact; and
- do not include aspects of Aboriginal society that are true of every society such as eating to survive.

Aboriginal Title

In general, "Aboriginal title" refers to the rights of Aboriginal Peoples to the occupation, use and enjoyment of their land and its resources. The classic legal definition was provided by the Supreme Court of Canada in *Delgamuukw v. British Columbia*:[2]

"… aboriginal title encompasses the right to exclusive use and occupation of land; second, aboriginal title encompasses the right to choose to what uses land can be put, subject to the ultimate limit that those uses cannot destroy the ability of the land to sustain future generations of Aboriginal Peoples; and third, that lands held pursuant to aboriginal title have an inescapable economic component." (at para. 166, emphasis in original)

Band

The *Indian Act* defines "band," in part, as a body of Indians for whose use and benefit in common, lands have been set apart. Each band has its own governing band council, usually consisting of a chief and several councillors. The members of the band usually share common values, traditions and practices rooted in their language and ancestral heritage. Today, many bands prefer to be known as First Nations.

Band chief

Someone elected by band members to govern for a specified term.

Band council or First Nation council

The band's governing body. Community members choose the chief and councillors by election under section 74 of the *Indian Act*, or through traditional custom. The band council's powers vary with each band.

Chinook Jargon

Describes a language that was loosely based on the Chinook Peoples' language. It developed as a trade language so that communication could take place between people who spoke different languages. It appeared in the 19th century from the Columbia River area and spread out into Washington, Oregon, British Columbia, and Alaska.

Elder

A man or woman whose wisdom about spirituality, culture and life is recognized and affirmed by the community. Not all Elders are old; sometimes the spirit of the Creator chooses to imbue a young Indigenous person. The Indigenous community and individuals will normally seek the advice and assistance of Elders in a wide range of traditional and contemporary issues.

First Nation

A term that came into common usage in the 1970s to replace the term "Indian band" which many found offensive. The term "First Nation" has been adopted to replace the word band in the name of many communities and can refer to a single band, many bands, an Indigenous governing body, something which is organized and established by an Indigenous community, or an Indigenous community as a whole.

Hereditary chief

A hereditary chief is a leader who has power passed down from one generation to the next along blood lines or other cultural protocols, similar to European royalty.

Impacts and Benefits Agreements (IBAS)

A broad term used to describe various contractual commitments related to development of land or resources subject to Aboriginal rights. IBAS usually impose negotiated limits on a project's impacts on the environment, on fish and wildlife, on the land and First Nations traditional use and enjoyment of same; and IBAS usually define a range of negotiated economic and preferential benefits to flow to the First Nation(s) whose lands are to be impacted by the development.

Indian

The term "Indian" may have different meanings, depending on context. Under the *Indian Act*, Indian means "a person who pursuant to this Act is registered as an Indian or is entitled to be registered as an Indian." There are a number of terms employing the term "Indian" including Status Indian, non-Status Indian, and Treaty Indian. Status Indians are those who are registered as Indians under the *Indian Act*, although some would include those who, although not registered, are entitled to be registered. Non-Status Indians are those who lost their status or whose ancestors were never registered or lost their status under former or current provisions of the *Indian Act*. Treaty Indians are those members of a community whose ancestors signed a treaty with the Crown and as a result are entitled to treaty benefits.

Indian Act

The *Indian Act* is federal legislation that regulates Indians and reserves and sets out certain federal government powers and responsibilities toward First Nations and their reserved lands. The first *Indian Act* was passed in 1876, although there were a number of pre-Confederation and post-Confederation enactments with respect to Indians and reserves prior to 1876. Since then, it has undergone numerous amendments, revisions and re-enactments. Indigenous and Northern Affairs Canada administers the *Indian Act*.

Indigenous Peoples

A. "Peoples in independent countries whose social, cultural and economic conditions distinguish them from other sections of the national community, and whose status is regulated wholly or partially by their own customs or traditions or by special laws or regulations";

B. "Peoples in independent countries who are regarded as indigenous on account of their descent from the populations which inhabited the country, or a geographical region to which the country belongs, at the time of conquest or colonization or the establishment of present state boundaries and who, irrespective of their legal status, retain some or all of their own social, economic, cultural and political institutions."[3]

Inuit

Indigenous people in northern Canada, living mainly in Nunavut, Northwest Territories, northern Quebec and Labrador. Ontario has a very small Inuit population. The Inuit are not covered by the *Indian Act*. The federal government has entered into several major land claim settlements with the Inuit.

Inukshuk vs Inuksuk

Inuksuk is the Inuit pronunciation and Inukshuk is the English translation. They are human-made stone landmarks used in the Arctic region of North America, as well as Greenland.

Métis

People of mixed Indian and European ancestry. The Métis history and culture draws on diverse ancestral origins such as Scottish, Irish, French, Ojibway and Cree. The Supreme Court of Canada in *R. v. Powley*[4] while not setting out a comprehensive definition of Métis for all purposes did set out the basic means to identify Métis rights-holders.

The Court identified three broad factors of self-identification, ancestral connection to the historic Métis community, and community acceptance.

Self-identification requires an individual to self-identify as a member of a Métis community not only to self-identify as Métis. Ancestral connection does not require a "blood quantum," but rather requires that an individual have some proof of an ancestral connection to the historic Métis community whose collective rights they are exercising. Community acceptance requires an individual to prove that a modern Métis community accepts that individual's Métis identity.

Midden site

A midden site is a place where Indigenous People placed their clam shells after consumption. Archaeologists count the layers of clam shells to see how long and how many people lived in the area.

Pictograph

Pictures that represent an object or an idea. Commonly used to refer to prehistoric paintings and drawings on rock walls.

Reserve

Defined by the *Indian Act* as "... tract of land, the legal title to which is vested in Her Majesty, that has been set apart by Her Majesty for the use and benefit of a band." A result of the definition of reserve land in the *Indian Act* is that reserve land cannot be privately owned by the band or band members.

Socio-Economic Participation Agreement (SEPA)

A synonym for Impacts and Benefits Agreement.

Traditional Ecological Knowledge (TEK)

TEK broadly describes systems for understanding one's environment, based on detailed personal observation and experience, and informed by generations of elders. TEK is recognized and used around the world as an important environmental assessment tool.

Traditional Territory

The geographic area identified by a First Nation to be the area of land which they and/or their ancestors traditionally occupied or used.

Treaty

An agreement between government and a First Nation that defines the rights of Aboriginal Peoples with respect to lands and resources over a specified area, and may also define the self-government authority of a First Nation.

Treaty Rights

Rights specified in a treaty. Rights to hunt and fish in traditional territory and to use and occupy reserves are typical treaty rights. This concept can have different meanings depending upon the context and perspective of the user.

Tribal Council

Not defined under the *Indian Act,* a Tribal Council usually represents a group of bands to facilitate the administration and delivery of local services to their members.

Usufructuary Rights

Communal or community rights to share in the use of property. This concept has been used by the courts in attempting to distinguish between Crown title and Aboriginal title.

NOTES

NOTES ON TERMINOLOGY

1 Strategic Alliance for Broadcasters for Aboriginal Reflection

PART I: INDIGENOUS AWARENESS

A. PRE CONTACT NATIONS

1 Sam Metcalfe, personal communication with staff of the Royal Commission on Aboriginal Peoples, 2 February 1995, *Report of the Royal Commission on Aboriginal Peoples,* Volume 4, page 108, 1996. Reproduced with the permission of the Minister of Public Works and Government Services, 2007, and Courtesy of the Privy Council Office.

2 *Delgamuukw v. British Columbia* [1997] 3 S.C.R. 1010

3 XÁ:YTEM Longhouse Interpretive Centre, 35087 Lougheed Highway, Mission, British Columbia, Canada

4 Weirs were used to pen turtles and fish. Corrals were used to pen land animals.

5 Gordon Mohs is an anthropologist who worked previously with the Sto:lo Nation and has extensively studied the Kwantlen First Nations People. For further information see: Gordon Mohs, *9,000 Years in the Valley of the Stone People*, Heritage B.C. Newsletter Winter (1996/97) 12-13.

6 Also known by the French term, Iroquois.

7 Wright, Ronald, *Stolen Continents: The "New World" Through Indian Eyes* (Toronto: Penguin Books, 1993) 4.

8 R. E. Gosnell's Digital Yearbook of British Columbia and Manual of Provincial Information 1901-2001 website at hp.bccna.bc.ca/Library/Yearbook/home.html which has digitally reproduced Gosnell, R.E., *The YearBook of British Columbia and Manual of Provincial Information, To Which is Added a Chapter Containing Much Special Information Respecting the Canadian Yukon and Northern Territory Generally.* Victoria, B.C.: (Government of British Columbia), 1897 [ie., 1901]. 406p. Cover stamped "1897 to 1901"

9 A full discussion of the importance of the *Royal Proclamation* is upcoming

10 For an excellent discussion, see: Aniel Raunet *Without Surrender, Without Consent: A History of the Nisga'a Land Claims* (Vancouver/Toronto: Douglas & McIntyre, 1996, Second Edition) 17-25.

11 This is often considered by researchers as a highly conservative estimate. A definitive population count at contact is not available.

12 *Calder v. Attorney-General of British Columbia*, [1973] S.C.R. 313

13 The Supreme Court of Canada in *R. v. Powley*, [2003] 2 S.C.R. 207, 2003 SCC 43 while not setting out a comprehensive definition of Métis for all purposes did set out the basic means to identify Métis rights-holders. See the Glossary for more details about the Powley decision

14 The Company kept control of just 6 million of the 120 million acres stretching from Fort Garry to the Rocky Mountains.

15 Riel remained a powerful political force in exile; he was elected three times to the House of Commons in absentia. Once he snuck into Ottawa to sign the Members' Register in the House, barely escaping with his life.

B. 1867-NATIONS TO WARDS

1   Ibid

2   It is important to recognize that while British Columbia's entry into Confederation in 1871 brought Section 91(24) into play, there were still many areas where the Province could (and did) use its jurisdiction to restrict Native ability to organize and act politically. For example, in 1872 British Columbia prohibited Indigenous Peoples from voting in provincial elections.

3   Public Archives of Canada, RG 10, Vol. 37 10, file 19,550-3. Hayter Reed to Edgar Dewdney, 20 July 1885.

4   Carter, Sarah. *A Lost Harvests: Prairie Indian Reserve Farmers and Government Policy* (Montreal & Kingston, London, Ithaca: McGill-Queen's University Press, 1990) 15.

5   Bateman, Rebecca. *Talking with The Plow: Agricultural Policy and Indian Farming in the Canadian and U.S. Prairies*

6   *An Act to amend The Indian Act, 1880*

7   *Canadian Charter of Rights and Freedoms*, Part 1 of the *Constitution Act, 1982,* being Schedule B to the *Canada Act 1982* (U.K.), 1982, c.11.

8   *Report of the Royal Commission on Aboriginal Peoples*, Volume 4, page 37, 1996. Reproduced with the permission of the Minister of Public Works and Government Services, 2007, and Courtesy of the Privy Council Office.

9   Historical Development of the Indian Act, Treaties and Historical Research Centre, P.R.E. Group, Indian and Northern Affairs, 1978

10 Judge Alfred Scow, Royal Commission of Aboriginal Peoples (RCAP), *Transcriptions of Public Hearings and Round Table Discussions, 1992-1993*

11 Statement of Apology, www.aadnc-aandc.gc.ca/eng/11001000015644. Reproduced with the permission of the Minister of Public Works and Government Services Canada, 2012.

12 Of these 12,000 Indigenous Peoples, approximately 7,000 were Status Indians. In this I will use the term Status Indian to refer to those Aboriginal Peoples who served in the military, and consequently lost their status under the Indian Act.

13 We would like to acknowledge that this article was framed from the research and writing of authors Maureen Lux (*Separate Beds A History of Indian Hospitals in Canada, 1920s–1980s*) and Gary Geddes (*Medicine Unbundled A Journey Through the Minefields of Indigenous Health Care*).

14 TB and Aboriginal People, CPHA, Canadian Public Health Leader; http://www.cpha.ca/en/programs/history/achievements/02-id/tb-aboriginal.aspx

15 Lux, Maureen Bacille de Calmette-Guérin, or BCG Vaccine for Tuberculosis; http://activehistory.ca/2015/03/bacille-de-calmette-guerin-or-bcg-vaccine-for-tuberculosis/

16 Alia, Valerie, *Names and Nunavut: Culture and Identity in the Inuit Homeland* (New York, Oxford: Berghahn Books, 2007) 20.

17 Roberts, Barry, A. *Eskimo Identification and Disc Numbers, A Brief History, Prepared for the Social Development Division, Department of Indian and Northern Affairs*, 1975, 20–21.

18 Canada's Relationship with Inuit: A History of Policy and Program Development, Indigenous and NorthernAffairs Canada website.

C. 1982—WARDS TO NATIONS

1   *Constitution Act, 1982*, being Schedule B to the *Canada Act 1982* (U.K.), 1982, c. 11.

2   *Calder v. Attorney-General of British Columbia*, [1973] S.C.R. 313

3   By the Treaty of Oregon, the United States gave up control of Vancouver Island to Britain in 1846.

4   *Guerin v. The Queen*, [1984] 2 S.C.R. 335

5   *MacMillan Bloedel Ltd. v. Mullin; Martin v. R. in Right of B.C.* (1985) 61 B.C.L.R. 145 (B.C.C.A.).

6   The key issue for the Nuu-chah-nulth was their desire to preserve evidence of their historic use of the natural resources of the area—they argued that clear-cut logging would erase that evidence.

7   *Martin*, Ibid., 160 (B.C.CA)

8   Supra, 172-173

9   Frank Calder was named B.C.'s Minister of Native Affairs, becoming Canada's first Aboriginal cabinet minister.

10 *R. v. Sparrow* [1990] S.C.R. 1075.

11 *Constitution Act, 1982*, being Schedule B to the *Canada Act 1982* (U.K.), 1982, c. 11

12 *Delgamuukw v. British Columbia* [1997] 3 S.C.R. 1010

13 *Haida Nation v. British Columbia (Minister of Forests)*, 2004 SCC 73

14 The Court transcript covered 369 days of proceedings.

15 "Notwithstanding the challenges created by the use of oral histories as proof of historical facts, the laws of evidence must be adapted in order that this type of evidence can be accommodated and placed on an equal footing with the types of historical evidence that courts are familiar with, which largely consists of historical documents." *Delgamuukw*, at Para 87

16 *R. v. Sparrow*, [1990] 1 S.C.R 1075

17 *Delgamuukw*, para. 168

18 *Delgamuukw*, para. 169

19 *Haida Nation v. British Columbia (Minister of Forests)* 2004 SCC 73

20 *Haida Nation*, paras. 16-17

21 *Haida Nation*, para. 35

22 *Haida Nation*, paras. 36-37

23 *Haida Nation*, paras. 42-48

24 *Haida Nation*, para. 53

25 *Haida Nation*, para 56

26 *Haida Nation*, para. 59

27 *Taku River Tlingit First Nation v. British Columbia (Project Assessment Director)*, 2004 SCC 74

28 *R. v. Powley*, 2003 SCC 43

29 Mikisew Cree First Nation v. Canada (Minister of Canadian Heritage), 2005 SCC 69

30 Ibid

31 Ibid, paras. 64-67

32 Ibid, para. 64

33 Ibid, paras. 65-66

34 *R. v. Marshall; R. v. Bernard*, [2005] 2 S.C.R. 220, 2005 SCC 43

35 The European concept of land ownership was foreign to Aboriginal Peoples. They believed that the land belonged to the Creator and that all Aboriginal Peoples were given the right to use and benefit from the land.

36 *R. v. Marshall; R. v. Bernard*, [2005] 2 S.C.R. 220, 2005 SCC 43, Paras. 134-135

37 *Rio Tinto Alcan Inc. v. Carrier Sekani Tribal Council*, 2010 SCC 43

38 Ibid, para. 31

39 Ibid, para. 53

40 Ibid, para. 83

41 *West Moberly First Nations v. British Columbia (Chief Inspector of Mines)* 2011 BCCA 247

42 Ibid, p. 237

43 *Tsilhqot'in Nation v. British Columbia* 2014 SCC 44, [2014] 2 S.C.R. 256

D. NEGOTIATING MODERN TREATIES AND OTHER AGREEMENTS

1 www.indianclaims.ca

2 B.C.'s modern era of treaty-making actually began in the fall of 1990, with then Premier Vander Zalm's announcement that his government was prepared to open negotiations with B.C.'s Aboriginal leaders (without acknowledging the existence of unextinguished Aboriginal title). On December 3, 1990, the British Columbia Claims Task Force was established. Made up of representatives of the federal and provincial governments and the First Nations Congress (later renamed the First Nations Summit—(FNS)), the Task Force presented its formal report on June 28, 1991, outlining 19 recommendations for treaty negotiation principles and procedures.

On September 21, 1992, representatives of the two orders of government and FNS signed the British Columbia Treaty Commission Agreement, endorsing all 19 Task Force recommendations—which included the formation of the British Columbia Treaty Commission and the establishment of a six stage treaty negotiation process.

3 www.ainc-AANDC.gc.ca/pr/pub/sg/plcy_e.html

4 Supra

5 To read the full text see: http://caid.ca/AFNBilAgr2005.pdf

E. SELF-RELIANCE THROUGH TREATIES AND OTHER SETTLEMENTS

1 *ABORIGINAL SELF-GOVERNMENT: The Government of Canada's Approach to Implementation of the Inherent Right and the Negotiation of Aboriginal Self-Government*, www.aadnc-aandc.gc.ca/eng/1100100031843/1100100031844

2 *Report of the Royal Commission on Aboriginal Peoples,* Volume 5, page 1, 1996. Reproduced with the permission of the Minister of Public Works and Government Services, 2007, and Courtesy of the Privy Council Office.

3 *Delgamuukw*, para. 186

4 *Report of the Royal Commission on Aboriginal Peoples*, Volume 5, page 1, 1996. Reproduced with the permission of the Minister of Public Works and Government Services, 2007, and Courtesy of the Privy Council Office.

5 Testimony before the RCAP, Lynn Brooks, Executive Director, Status of Women Council of the N.W.T., Yellowknife, Northwest Territories, 7 December, 1992. *Report of the Royal Commission on Aboriginal Peoples*, Volume 4, page 75-76, 1996. Reproduced with the permission of the Minister of Public Works and Government Services, 2007, and Courtesy of the Privy Council Office.

6 *Report of the Royal Commission on Aboriginal Peoples,* Volume 5, page 56, 1996. Reproduced with the permission of the Minister of Public Works and Government Services, 2007, and Courtesy of the Privy Council Office.

7 *Calder v. Attorney-General of British Columbia*, [1973] S.C.R. 313

8 *Federal Policy Guide*: *ABORIGINAL SELF-GOVERNMENT*—*The Government of Canada's Approach to Implementation of the Inherent Right and the Negotiation of Aboriginal Self-Government*, Ibid., 3

10 *Campbell et al. v.* AG *B.C./*AG *Cda & Nisga'a Nation et al,* paras. 168-171

11 *Federal Policy Guide:* ABORIGINAL SELF-GOVERNMENT—*The Government of Canada's Approach to Implementation of the Inherent Right and the Negotiation of Aboriginal Self-Government,* Ibid., 3

12 Supra, 4

13 Supra, 5

14 Supra, 5 The Policy Guide goes on to spell out that, in these areas, "primary law-making authority would remain with the federal or provincial governments, as the case may be, and their laws would prevail in the event of a conflict with Aboriginal laws."

15 Supra, 4

16 *Sechelt Indian Band Self-Government Act,* S.C. 1986, c. 27

17 *Report of the Royal Commission on Aboriginal Peoples,* Volume 4, page 436, 1996. Reproduced with the permission of the Minister of Public Works and Government Services, 2007, and Courtesy of the Privy Council Office.

18 *Nisga'a Final Agreement Act,* S.C. 2000, c. 7

F. INDIGENOUS PEOPLES: THEN AND NOW

1   As mentioned earlier, we use the term "Indigenous Peoples" to indicate the uniqueness and diversity of the various First Nation, Inuit, and Métis peoples who live in Canada, with their different histories, traditions, values, beliefs, and aspirations. We use the term "Aboriginal Peoples" to indicate the collective group of people who hold various rights and obligations under provisions of the *Indian Act* and the Canadian *Constitution,* to which the general public are not subject.

2   In 2017 around 200 First Nations in Canada hold elections under s. 74 of the *Act*

3   Robert P.C. Joseph's father is a hereditary Chief.

4   Aboriginal Peoples in Canada: First Nations People, Métis and Inuit http://www12.statcan.gc.ca/nhs-enm/2011/as-sa/99-011-x/99-011-x2011001-eng.cfm#bx2

5   Ibid

6   ibid

7   *Report of the Royal Commission on Aboriginal Peoples,* Volume 4, page 538, 1996. Reproduced with the permission of the Minister of Public Works and Government Services, 2007, and Courtesy of the Privy Council Office.

8   Aboriginal Peoples in Canada: First Nations People, Métis and Inuit, http://www12.statcan.gc.ca/nhs-enm/2011/as-sa/99-011-x/99-011-x2011001-eng.cfm#bx2

9   Ibid

10 Ibid

11 Fact Sheet—2011 National Household Survey Aboriginal Demographics, Educational Attainment and Labour Market Outcomes www.aadnc-aandc.gc.ca/eng/1376329205785/1376329233875

12 The full version of the Declaration on the Rights of Indigenous Peoples can be found at: www.un.org/esa/socdev/unpfii/documents/DRIPS_en.pdf

13 *Report of the Royal Commission on Aboriginal Peoples,* Volume 2, page 422-423, 1996. Reproduced with the permission of the Minister of Public Works and Government Services, 2007, and Courtesy of the Privy Council Office.

PART 11: WORKING EFFECTIVELY WITH INDIGENOUS PEOPLES
A. THE BUSINESS CASE FOR WORKING EFFECTIVELY WITH INDIGENOUS PEOPLES®

1   Canadian Business for Social Responsibility provides both an excellent overview and in-depth discussion. See: www.cbsr.ca

2   For example, in 1999 the Dow Jones Index Sustainability Index (DJSI) became the world's first major financial index to monitor the performance of leading companies against an array of "CSR" indicators. Dow Jones reports that the leading global companies on their DJSI consistently produce financial results superior to those reported on their conventional Dow Jones Index. See: www.sustainability-index.com

3   The Vancouver Organizing Committee for the 2010 Olympic and Paralympic Winter Games (VANOC) designed its procurement protocol to ensure Indigenous involvement and sustainability-based practices. http://www.collectionscanada.gc.ca/obj/thesescanada/vol2/BVAU/TC-BVAU-28120.pdf

4   In 1995, the federal government affirmed its commitment to treaty-making by publishing its formal Policy Guide, *ABORIGINAL SELF-GOVERNMENT: The Government of Canada's Approach to Implementation of the Inherent Right and the Negotiation of Indigenous Self-Government,* which stated: "The Government of Canada recognizes the inherent right of self-government as an existing aboriginal right under section 35 of the *Constitution Act, l982*. It recognizes, as well, that the inherent right may find expression in treaties..."

5   The First Nations Tax Commission is responsible for ensuring the First Nations tax system is administratively efficient, harmonized, improves economic growth, and is responsive to on-reserve taxpayers. See: www.fntc.ca

6   For example, bilateral negotiations between Westbank First Nation and the federal government opened in 1990. The *Westbank First Nation Self-Government Act* was passed by Parliament on May 6, 2004. In June, 2005, the Government of British Columbia and Westbank First Nation reached agreement regarding the building of a major new bridge across Lake Okanagan to link Westbank and Kelowna.

7   The *Westbank First Nation Self-Government Act* was passed by Parliament on May 6, 2004, approving the *Westbank First Nation Self-Government Agreement*. In June, 2005, the Government of British Columbia and Westbank First Nation reached agreement regarding the building of a major new bridge across Lake Okanagan to link Westbank and Kelowna.

8   Canadian Business for Social Responsibility provides both an excellent overview and in-depth discussion. See: www.cbsr.ca

9   See: British Columbia News Release 2005ARR0011-001135 https://archive.news.gov.bc.ca/releases/news_releases_2005-2009/2005ARR0011-001135.pdf

10 For more information regarding property tax reforms to assist First Nations to generate revenues see: http://www.aadnc-aandc.gc.ca/eng/1322671345976

11 Section 87 *Indian Act* issues see: www.laws-lois.justice.gc.ca/eng/acts/i-5/page-12.html#docCont

12 For example, Bill C-23 The First Nations Statistical and Management Act.

13 The First Nations Tax Commission is responsible for ensuring the First Nations property tax system is administratively efficient, harmonized, improves economic growth, and is responsive to on-reserve taxpayers. See: www.fntc.ca

14 The 1968 Summer Olympic Games in Mexico City were marked by the famous "Black Power" salutes of two American sprinters during their Medal Presentation Ceremony seen and repeated countless times on television around the world. See: http://www.historylearningsite.co.uk/the-civil-rights-movement-in-america-1945-to-1968/mexico-1968/

15 For a more extensive list, see Section C RESPECT: A Path toward *Working Effectively with Indigenous Peoples®*, Do and Don't—A Checklist

B. ABORIGINAL CONSULTATION

1   See "1982—Wards to Nations" for discussion of the leading case: *Haida Nation v. British Columbia (Minister of Forests)*, 2004 SCC 73

2   *Haida*, Ibid., para. 53

3   See "Chapter "C 1982—Wards to Nations"

4   www.amnesty.ca/our-work/issues/indigenous-peoples/indigenous-peoples-in-canada/grassy-narrows

5   *Constitution Act, 1982*, being Schedule B to the *Canada Act 1982* (U.K.), 1982, c. 11 Canada's Constitutional guarantee of "aboriginal and treaty rights." For discussion, please refer to "Chapter C 1982—Wards to Nations"

6   *Haida Nation*, Ibid., paras. 16-17

7   Supra, paras. 32-34

8   Supra, para. 35

9   For example, the Tahltan First Nation found itself handling hundreds of Referrals and was participating in a number of Environmental Assessment processes all at the same time. For any size of community this can strain administration resources beyond their capacity.

C. RESPECT: A PATH TOWARD WORKING EFFECTIVELY WITH INDIGENOUS PEOPLES®

1   For an excellent discussion of the distinctiveness and diversity of "peoples" signified by the use of the phrase "Indian, Inuit and Métis peoples of Canada" in section 35 of *The Constitution Act, 1982*, see: *Report of the Royal Commission on Aboriginal Peoples* Volume 4, Appendix 5A

2   For discussion, see *Report of the Royal Commission on Aboriginal Peoples*, Volume 4, Chapter 2: *Women's Perspectives*, 43-53; and Chapter 7: *Urban Perspectives*, 519-621

3   *Delgamuukw*, Ibid., at Para 87

"Notwithstanding the challenges created by the use of oral histories as proof of historical facts, the laws of evidence must be adapted in order that this type of evidence can be accommodated and placed on an equal footing with the types of historical evidence that courts are familiar with, which largely consists of historical documents."

GLOSSARY

1   *Haida Nation v. British Columbia (Minister of Forests)* 2004 SCC 73, Paragraphs 40-56

2   [1997] 3 S.C.R. 1010

3   A number of definitions are in use; this widely recognized definition comes from ILO 169, a respected international convention.

4   *R. v. Powley*, [2003] 2 S.C.R. 207, 2003 SCC 43

INDEX

ABOUT THE AUTHORS

Bob Joseph, founder of Indigenous Corporate Training Inc., has provided training on Indigenous and Aboriginal relations since 1994. As a certified Master Trainer, Bob has assisted both individuals and organizations in building Indigenous or Aboriginal relations. His Canadian clients include all levels of government, Fortune 500 companies, financial institutions, including the World Bank, small and medium-sized corporate enterprises, and Indigenous peoples. He has worked internationally for clients in the United States, Guatemala, Peru, and New Caledonia in the South Pacific. In 2006, Bob co-facilitated a worldwide Indigenous Peoples' round table in Switzerland, which included participants from the United Nations, Australia, New Zealand, North, Central and South America, Africa, and the Philippines.

In May 2001, Bob was profiled in an annual feature called "Training: the New Guard 2001" by the American Society of Training and Development (ASTD) in their prestigious magazine, *T + D*. Bob was one of nine trainers selected for the feature from over 70,000 members who come from more than 100 countries and 15,000 organizations.

Bob additionally has worked as an associate professor at Royal Roads University. He has an educational background in business administration and international trade. As an author and co-author, Bob has contributed to a number of resources relating to working with Aboriginal or Indigenous Peoples. He also manages a blog called *Working Effectively with Indigenous Peoples®*, which is a resource that supports people in their Indigenous relations endeavours.

Bob Joseph is an Indigenous person, or more specifically a Status Indian, and is a member of the Gwawaenuk Nation. The Gwawaenuk is one of the many Kwakwaka'wakw tribes located between Comox and Port Hardy on Vancouver Island and the adjacent mainland of British Columbia. He comes from a proud potlatch family and is an initiated member of the Hamatsa Society. As the son of a hereditary chief, he will one day, in accordance with strict cultural laws, become a hereditary chief.

Cynthia F. Joseph is an integral part of the Indigenous Corporate Training Inc team. She is co-author of our books and is the main developer of the on-line training programs.

Cindy received her Bachelor of Laws degree from the University of British Columbia in 1990 and was called to the bar in 1991. She maintained a general law practice consecutively on the North Shore of Vancouver, Bowen Island, and Burnaby to retire from law in Port Coquitlam.

While maintaining a legal practice Cindy began using her experiences as a faculty member at Capilano University in the highly recognized Paralegal Program. The combination of her legal degree and her experience providing instruction in class, and in a virtual format have been invaluable in developing the online training programs that we offer. Cindy's research skills and educational background ensure that our *Working Effectively with Indigenous Peoples®* books and training manuals are up to date and reliable.

ADDITIONAL INFORMATION

"Bob talks fast & provides an insight in every breath. Make sure you come with an empty mind because it will be full when you're done."—C.H.

INDIGENOUS CORPORATE TRAINING INC. (ICT) is a global training company committed to working collaboratively with regional, national, and international clients to provide a broad range of performance improvement training services geared specifically at helping individuals and organizations work effectively with Indigenous Peoples. We at ICT recognize that organizations and their shareholders are interested in demonstrated results of how performance improvement consulting expenditures contribute to the effectiveness of an organization. We go to great lengths to ensure there is a demonstrated link between performance improvement consulting measures and increased organizational effectiveness. ICT knows that funds spent on performance improvement training are at the expense of other initiatives, and we understand that the performance improvement must be the main driver of the work we do.

Our *Working Effectively with Indigenous Peoples®* training has been delivered to Fortune 500 companies, financial institutions, including the World Bank, small and medium sized corporate enterprises, and through all levels of governments across Canada. It has also been delivered in North and South America, and Switzerland.

ICT provides public and on-site training. Our schedule for public and virtual training sessions is posted on **www.ictinc.ca**. To arrange for on-site training, please contact our office at **info@ictinc.ca**.

If you would like additional information and opportunities to learn and share ideas with others subscribe to our free, monthly newsletter. In the newsletter you will find a variety of information to enhance your understanding of *Working Effectively with Indigenous Peoples®*. Visit our blog and sign up for our newsletter at **www.ictinc.ca/blog**.